Alex Rawlings is a language s[...] experience teaching, coaching [...] multiple different languages. He [...] Multilingual Student after being t[...] different languages aged twenty and since then has gone on to study many more, including Russian, Hebrew and Hungarian. Alex has taken part in nationwide campaigns to promote multilingualism, has contributed to blogs run by the British Council and the European Commission, and his skills have been featured by news and media outlets in countries around the world. He is an organiser of the annual Polyglot Conference.

How to Speak Any Language Fluently

Alex Rawlings

A How To Book

ROBINSON

First published in Great Britain in 2017
by Robinson

3 5 7 9 10 8 6 4 2

p1: Quotation by Kató Lomb reproduced
courtesy of TESL-EJ.

A CIP catalogue record for this book
is available from the British Library.

ISBN: 978-1-47213-856-9

Typeset in Sentinel by SX Composing DTP,
Rayleigh, Essex
Printed and bound in Great Britain by
CPI Group (UK) Ltd, Croydon CR0 4YY

Robinson
An imprint of
Little, Brown Book Group
Carmelite House
50 Victoria Embankment
London EC4Y 0DZ

An Hachette UK Company
www.hachette.co.uk

www.littlebrown.co.uk

How To Books are published by
Robinson, an imprint of Little, Brown
Book Group. We welcome proposals
from authors who have first-hand
experience of their subjects.
Please set out the aims of your book,
its target market and its suggested
contents in an email to
Nikki.Read@howtobooks.co.uk.

Contents

Introduction

'*A nyelv az egyetlen, amit rosszul is érdemes tudni.*'
(Language is the only thing worth knowing even poorly.)
Kató Lomb (1909–2003)
Hungarian translator and polyglot

Languages are one of those unique things in life that are always worth learning. Whether you know a lot or just a little, whether you speak them every day or once a year, and whether you speak many or just one, you are better off for knowing what you do than if you didn't know it at all. Even just a few words in a foreign language are better than knowing nothing at all.

Kató Lomb was one of the greatest language learners that the world has ever known. Including her native Hungarian, she worked as a translator in sixteen different languages and allegedly was able to speak many more to varying degrees of fluency. It is her quote that opens this introduction which has inspired me to learn languages more than any other. It is her non-perfectionist attitude to languages and desire to learn anything rather than nothing that I have tried to emulate in all areas of my life. Her outstanding success speaks for itself.

Being successful at learning languages is as much about the expectations you set yourself and the attitude you adopt as anything else. It is impossible to be a perfectionist in this sphere. You can score 100 per cent in tests, you can finish books and you can complete courses all you like, but no matter what milestone you reach, there will always be fresh ones appearing on the horizon.

Language learning never stops. No matter how much you know, there will always be more to learn. Nothing can change that, and the most successful language learners such as Kató Lomb recognise that and adjust accordingly, right from the start.

Learning a new language is an endlessly exciting and rewarding journey. As you set out on it, you can look forward to the exhilarating rush of learning new words, and the immense satisfaction of forming whole sentences and making yourself understood. These highs will always eclipse the lows, as you will realise one day that you can't imagine what life was like when you couldn't speak the language you're learning now.

The journey of learning a new language is a voyage of discovery. You will discover new cultures, new customs, and begin to see a whole new dimension of the world that you were blind to before. You will also gain new insights into human nature and humanity itself. You will meet people totally unlike anyone you've met before, and be able to connect with them in ways you never thought possible. But perhaps most importantly, you will discover a side of yourself that you never knew. You will learn how your mind works, why it remembers some things but not others, and what makes you motivated and what doesn't. Ultimately, a crucial segment of the journey of learning a new language is about learning how you learn.

At the time of writing, I have been dedicated to learning languages for just over ten years. I have studied fifteen different languages, and been on fifteen totally different adventures with them. Because of the experiences and opportunities each of these languages have brought me, I feel almost as though in those ten short years I have lived fifteen different lives.

At first, learning a new language was slow, it was frustrating, and it felt like an impossible task. I could never imagine what it would be like to feel confident enough to hold a conversation in a foreign language. I didn't really believe that I would ever experience that.

Thankfully, I carried on regardless. Time was on my side as I started very young, and I was fortunate to have multilingual role models in my family, such as my grandmother Aphroditi who was trilingual, and my great-aunt Gladys who spoke French, English, Greek, Arabic and Italian completely fluently. In the later stages of her life it became necessary to know bits of all of these to talk to her, as she started mixing them all into her sentences and was not always aware that she was switching language mid-sentence. She told me that for her 'Chaque langue est une autre personalité.' (Each language is a different personality.) Each of the languages she spoke was a part of the story of her life, and by mixing them in her speech, she was defining who she was.

Through experience and with patience, I gradually found ways to make the way I learned languages more efficient, and better suited to me. This allowed me to learn languages faster, but also retain them in the longer term. As a language teacher and coach, I had the chance to experiment and see how my techniques could be adapted to suit people with different personality types to me, and start to see the commonalities between the approaches that worked for everyone. It is these commonalities that form the basis of this book.

Learning a new language is an extremely exciting, endlessly entertaining, and stimulating challenge. Whether you are looking for a way to start, or are in the middle of your journey and looking for ways forwards, this book will help you. It will offer fresh ideas, a wider perspective, and an overview of several different tried and tested techniques that will make your learning quicker, easier and much more enjoyable.

The process of learning a new language is inevitably a very personal process, which means that you may find that some techniques will agree with you more than others. This book is not designed to be an instruction manual, but a guide. The chapters are ordered logically, according to the kinds of questions that will arise as you progress through the different stages of learning your new language. However, it does not need to be read from cover to cover and can be dipped into as a reference whenever the need arises. The exercises at the end of each chapter will serve as a summary of the chapter's key points, and also give you some things to think about and consider as you apply the advice and techniques that it outlines.

As we will see, there are many different ways to learn a language. The aim of this book is to help you find yours.

Now let's get started!

CHAPTER 1

Getting Started

*Welcome to the world of learning languages.
Congratulations on taking up one of the most rewarding
and exciting challenges that life has to offer. Learning a new
language is a huge adventure. It takes you to places that you
have never been to. It opens doors for you that you never
knew were there. It introduces you to people that you would
otherwise have just walked by. And life certainly will never
seem the same again.*

A new language brings you a whole host of new opportunities.
It allows you to step into a parallel universe, where you get the
chance to live your life again but in a different language, inter-
acting with people from different countries in ways you never
could before.

But as with all things, the challenge of learning a new language brings difficulties with it too. The ability to speak a
foreign language is a skill that can be developed only through
patience, with dedication, and over time.

In this chapter we will see why learning a language is something everybody should be doing and can benefit from. We will
think about your choice of language, identify your reasons

why, and devise a plan of action to start you off towards your goals.

Ten Good Reasons Why Everybody Should Be Learning a Language

1. THE BRAIN GYM

Learning a new language keeps your brain active. It requires you to constantly be learning new things and applying your new knowledge. Each time you learn something new, neural pathways are formed in your brain that help keep it active and young. Spending a few minutes each day learning a new language is a bit like doing Sudoku, but infinitely more useful and applicable.

2. SEE THE WORLD DIFFERENTLY

Speaking a new language forces you to change the way in which you express yourself. You will learn new sayings, new expressions, and see how languages express ideas in entirely different ways. Gradually, you will develop a sense of how the people who speak your new language think. This will introduce you to a world that your native tongue alone could never have shown you.

3. EARN MORE MONEY

Studies suggest people who speak more languages can earn more money. In a globalised world, the ability to communicate with customers and colleagues in their own language is as invaluable to you as it is to your employer. There are also whole industries based exclusively around language skills, such as translation and interpretation, but also social media moderation, advertising, diplomacy, and many others.

4. GAIN INCREASED COGNITIVE ABILITIES

Science has proven that speaking a foreign language actually makes you smarter. It will speed up your brain, and allow it to process more complex information at the same time. Importantly, these benefits are available to anyone learning a foreign language at any time of their life, not just those brought up bilingual or multilingual.

DID YOU KNOW?

In an experiment, it was shown that babies who had simply *heard* more than one language before they had spoken their first word were able to focus on two different sources of light, while babies who had only heard one language could only focus on one at a time.

5. DELAY DEMENTIA BY 4.5 YEARS

Learning a new language is so good for your brain that scientists have now proven that doing so will delay the onset of dementia or Alzheimer's disease by about 4.5 years. This makes learning a language one of the most effective ways known to prevent the condition.

6. COPE WITH MENTAL HEALTH PROBLEMS

The NHS lists learning a new language as one of the best ways to deal with depression and other mental health conditions. Studying, plus the routine and regularity that it requires, is a great way to cope with these kinds of stresses in your life.

7. INCREASED CULTURAL AWARENESS

Learning a language brings you into contact with a huge range of different people and cultures that you might otherwise never have had the chance to get to know. Being able to speak to people in their own language gives you a unique opportunity to come to understand them, their views, beliefs and traditions. That in turn will make you more aware than ever before of both the differences and the similarities that exist between cultures. It is impossible to truly 'know' a culture different to your own without also knowing its language.

8. BUILD BETTER RELATIONSHIPS

Generally, people love speaking their own language. If you give them that chance, they will feel far freer and more open to speaking to you and getting to know you, than if you oblige them to speak your language. Nowadays, when it is almost expected that people will communicate in English, this is more true than ever, so that when someone *has* made the effort to learn another language, it really is well received. You will get better service on holidays, and even make friendships that could last a lifetime.

9. UNDERSTAND YOUR OWN LANGUAGE BETTER

Even though you speak your own language natively, you probably haven't spent much time thinking about it. Learning a new language will make you more aware of grammar, where words come from, expressions and how to write effectively, not just in the one you're learning, but in your native language too. You will find yourself much better placed to analyse grammar and use your native language more precisely and accurately.

10.LEARNING LANGUAGES IS A WAY OF LIFE!

Learning a new language is a lifelong undertaking. However much you know, there will always be more left to learn. As you start taking on a new language and getting to know a new culture and new people, you are likely to get hooked in the process. There is no pastime more mentally stimulating and satisfying than this.

Which Language Is for You?

Languages are not created equally. There are languages that take longer to learn than others. Some will be readily accessible to you, but others will make you work harder to find books and courses. Some will have grammar that you will recognise and learn quickly, while others will really make you work for it first.

Learning a new language is something very personal, and so it's hard to talk objectively about which language you should be learning. Your new language will have a considerable impact on your life, and so it is important to feel motivated and certain that you are making the right choice.

Whether or not you'll be successful in learning a new language is often simply a matter of choosing the right language from the beginning. If you're sure you've made the right choice, and sure not only that you want, but *need* to speak the language you're learning, that will motivate you and propel you through more challenging times and onwards towards achieving your long-term goals.

Before you set off on your language-learning journey, here are four crucial questions that you should ask:

1. WHO DO I KNOW THAT SPEAKS THIS?

Relationships are powerful motivators. Many people learn languages successfully for love, but equally having friends, relatives or colleagues who speak your chosen language can be motivating enough too. Do you know anyone who speaks this language, and how will your relationship with them improve by your learning it?

2. WILL SPEAKING THIS LANGUAGE HELP ME AT WORK?

If you have any upcoming projects, business trips or meetings in which you can use your new language, these can offer you something to aim for and focus on while studying and planning your learning. Think about new opportunities that this language could offer you, and how it could help you progress in your career.

3. WILL I USE THIS LANGUAGE TO TRAVEL?

The pilgrimage to the country where your chosen language is spoken is almost like a sacred, spiritual undertaking for any language learner. It gives you the chance to see months of hard work pay off as you find yourself able to speak to real people in their own language, and pride yourself on noticing how, as the days go past, you use less and less English. The prospect of travelling to the country of your target language is very exciting indeed, but it may not always be realistic for it to happen in the short term. Can you imagine yourself ever making your language-learning pilgrimage to that specific place? If not, is there another language you could be learning for which that seems more likely?

4. DO I LIKE THIS LANGUAGE'S CULTURE?

As you make further progress with your new language, it will become increasingly important to be interested in its culture. You should enjoy watching films, reading books and engaging with any of the language's cultural products. Culture is the soul of a language and makes the grammar tables and vocab lists you'll be learning feel human.

> ## TOP TIP: PLAN HOW YOU WILL *USE* IT
> Start looking for conversation groups, meetups, courses, language exchanges and anything that will allow you to speak the language you're learning where you live. If you can't find live events, you can always practise with people via Skype or social networks (see Chapter 9).

Set Objectives

Deciding that you want to speak a foreign language is a great start. The most important step, though, is deciding *how* you want to be able to speak it, and what you want to use it for. Have this clear in your mind from the very beginning, and then you can focus on streamlining your learning efforts to get you there as quickly as possible.

Picture yourself in a year's time. Ask yourself:

★   **Where** are you speaking the language?
★   **Whom** are you speaking it with?
★   **How** confident do you feel using it?
★   **What** kinds of things can you talk about?

Then you can start planning how you will build up to that over the next year, and start working towards your first steps and objectives.

A good, general first step is to aim to have basic conversations about everyday things, be able to introduce yourself, and interact with native speakers in a polite and friendly manner.

Depending on your circumstances, you may have more specific goals instead. You could aim to pass an exam, move abroad, or hold a conversation with your in-laws. The most crucial element of this is that it is personal to your objectives, and reasonable for your schedule.

Action Points

Your next step is to break your objectives down into smaller steps, or action points. Some of these you will be able to start working towards straight away!

Here's an example of an initial list:

★ Make room for study time in your routine.
★ Buy a course book.
★ Complete one unit/chapter per week.
★ Learn fifteen to twenty words each week.
★ Aim each week to do something that you couldn't do the week before.

If your long term objective is to learn to watch films and not have to rely on subtitles, you could work towards that goal as follows:

★ Watch thirty minutes of foreign TV per day and one film per week.

★ Write down all new words and phrases you hear, and learn them.

★ Aim by the next week to reduce the number of new words/phrases by 5 per cent.

★ Switch from subtitles in your language to subtitles in the language you're learning.

★ Start watching TV without any subtitles at all.

If you organise your learning in this way, it will be easier for you to keep track of the progress you're making and plan how to keep advancing towards your goals in the quickest and most efficient way possible.

Find Resources

With your objectives and action points in place, it's now time to start looking for resources that will help get you there.

Firstly, there is often an enormous amount of choice if you are learning a major language like French, German, Spanish, Chinese, etc. You should spend time researching different options and also experimenting with what you like best, and working out what you don't.

The key to making the right decision is to refer back to your objectives. If you want to speak and understand the spoken language more, you should be looking for courses with more audio and video materials. If, however, you want to focus on reading and writing, you will need a course that has more written material.

As part of your resources check, you should look for opportunities to speak the language too. This could be in the form of a weekly evening class at a local college, foreign language institute, or adult education centre, or even through working with a private teacher online or offline (see Chapter 3). Speaking from a very early stage is invaluable, as it helps to put everything you have been learning in theory into practice.

WHAT ABOUT SMALLER LANGUAGES?

If you are learning a less commonly learnt language, you may feel like you are bucking the trend slightly and as a result, that there are far fewer resources available. Ultimately, you will have to compromise and try to make the most out of what you can get. In this case, always complement your study time with plenty of speaking practice with a native speaker, to allow you to customise your learning and focus on what your objectives are.

When Your Motives Change

Learning a new language is a long and exciting journey. Along the way, the reasons why you first set out on that journey will adapt and change. This is natural and healthy, but means that you should be prepared to revisit your long-term objectives and adjust them accordingly.

You may start off planning a holiday somewhere, and so just aim to master basic phrases for restaurants, hotels and so on. While you're there, you may make new friends who you stay in touch with, and then find that your need for the language changes. More than just ordering your meal, you will now want to form a friendship and express your thoughts and feelings in the language, while also understanding theirs.

Another way of looking at this is that your initial objective was to reach an elementary level. Once you got there, you found fresh motivation to push on to an intermediate, and eventually an advanced level.

When you have reached your first objective, set fresh ones and create new action points to get there. Language learning really does never stop!

Exercises

1. Make a list of every language you have had contact with in the last month. Which of these are viable for you to learn, which aren't, and why?

2. Write a list of ten different reasons why you have chosen to learn your language.

3. Write down one or more long-term objectives for your new language, then break these down into feasible action points for you to start working towards straightaway.

4. Compile a list of all of the resources you have available, both online and offline. Work out how you are going to use these to your advantage.

5. Start keeping a progress log that you update once per week. Write in it how you are feeling, what went well this week, and what you would like to improve on for next week.

Model Answers: Person A

1. English (native), French (neighbours), Swahili (in the street), Italian (in the street), Czech (co-workers), **German (friends)**.

2.   a. Not rely on English when visiting Berlin
     b. Have an excuse to visit Berlin more often
     c. Understand German culture better
     d. Increase career prospects
     e. The intellectual challenge
     f. Impress friends and family with language skills
     g. Get to know German friends better
     h. Meet new people through courses
     i. The language sounds beautiful

3. Not to use any English on next trip to Berlin.

   Action points: Learn basic phrases (ordering food, directions, shops etc.)
                    Practise speaking once per week
                    Practise listening once per week
                    Practise answering unprepared questions

4. Coursebooks/textbooks (local library/bookshop), apps, podcasts, videos, online courses (internet), local German meet-up group in her town (organised through the internet, takes place in real life), German classes/private lessons (local language schools), Skype lessons/exchanges (internet).

5. Week 1
   This week, my priority was to find some resources that will enable me to speak less English on my next trip to Berlin. I've found some podcasts with the first episodes for free, and I took out a language-learning CD from my local library. I'm enjoying listening to these for 20–25 minutes each morning on my way to work. I try to

listen again when I get home so I can repeat some of the phrases. On Thursday evening, I spent a few minutes writing down some of the phrases I could remember before I played it again. I'm looking forward to making more progress, and by next week I'd like to remember most of the phrases from Unit 1 of the course on disc.

–fast forward–

<u>Week 8</u>
This week, I managed for the first time to have a full conversation with my teacher Mareike, who I found on a website. It was just basics like 'Where do you live?' and 'Do you like Birmingham?'. I stuttered a lot and definitely made loads of mistakes, but it felt good. An hour a week with Mareike on Skype has made a big difference. She's forcing me to practise things I wouldn't otherwise. She's encouraging and makes everything seem fun! I'm spending less time on listening exercises in the mornings and focusing more on practising vocab from my lessons with Mareike. Things have been hectic at work and I've been slacking a bit recently, so I've taken the plunge. I've booked flights to Berlin in six weeks' time! Now I'm definitely going to get cracking. Next week I'm aiming to have a longer conversation with Mareike, and I'll look up some questions to ask her and think of some answers.

CHAPTER 2

Using Your Time

Language learning never stops. No matter how much you know, there's always more to learn. Human nature means that you will probably never be fully satisfied with your level anyway. Silly mistakes will still keep popping up, even when you least expect it. You may still be revisited by that feeling when you start out saying something and words later realise you're missing the vocabulary you need to make any sense.

How Long Should It Take?

How long is a piece of string? There is no simple answer to how long it should take to learn a new language, and for a very good reason.

Thinking about learning a new language purely in terms of time is the wrong way to go about it. Learning a new language is a fun and exciting adventure and a rewarding hobby, that should be done without looking at the clock.

All of the suggested lengths of time that follow should only be seen as guidelines. You may reach these stages faster or slower than what is suggested here. That really depends on you, the language you're learning, and the circumstances surrounding your learning.

THREE MONTHS

★ Your first three months are when you'll feel most enthusiastic, and should expect to get the most done. This is a similar phenomenon to when people first start out on a diet and find that it is in the initial stages that they lose the most weight. If you study intensively in this time, e.g. every day at least once per day, you could reach the stage where you can start speaking. That doesn't mean you will be stringing together complex sentences of expressing profound thoughts, but you'll be on your way.

ONE YEAR

★ A year can be a long or a short time in terms of language learning. If you manage to keep up the momentum of your first three months, you stand a chance of getting quite far in this time. Most of us, however, start to tail off after the first few months, meaning that by the time of the one-year anniversary of learning your new language, you will have made good progress, but still have plenty of room for improvement.

A LIFETIME

★ Over the course of your life your language skills will fluctuate. At times they will get better, at times they will get worse. The only way to keep things fresh and make progress is to keep studying all the way through. Even if by the end you just do ten to fifteen minutes per week, you will stay on top of things.

How Much Time Do You Need?

Learning a new language should not and – in the long term – cannot take up all of your time. You should still be able to work a full-time job, raise a family, go to the supermarket, and do household chores.

The aim is not to drop your life in order to learn languages. Instead, you want to make languages a key and unmissable aspect of what you do that it becomes part of your daily life.

The amount of time you should aim to spend learning languages each day will vary, depending on your level. In an ideal scenario, you would be able to spend one hour per day studying, especially when you are starting out and still have lots of enthusiasm. But within that hour, there is plenty of room for flexibility.

Committing to an hour does not mean sitting down for one single block each day. Your time will be far better spent if instead you break that time up into smaller chunks that you scatter out around your day. It is far easier to motivate yourself to do shorter bursts than long periods of study. It also keeps your brain refreshed and makes it easier for you to absorb information over the course of the day, as you keep reminding yourself of it. Finally, if something comes up and you have to miss one of these sessions, at least you have the others that day to make up for it.

The 15/30/15 Routine

Break your hour down into three main slots: fifteen minutes at breakfast, thirty minutes at lunchtime, and fifteen minutes around the time you eat in the evening. Use these as follows:

FIFTEEN MINUTES A.M. – REVIEW #2

★ Look over your notes from the night before and see how much you remember after a night's sleep. Anything that is still causing problems should continue to be prioritised at in the following sessions.

THIRTY MINUTES MIDDAY – STUDY TIME

★ Your longer session should be used for learning new information and moving further along with your course and study materials. You can also use this time to do homework and exercises. This time should feel focused and productive.

FIFTEEN MINUTES P.M. – REVIEW #1

★ This is your first chance to look back at what you covered at midday. Make sure the rules and vocabulary you learned are all still fresh in your head, and try again to learn the ones that have been missing. The next morning, you will get a chance to review again.

This rhythm works best when done every day, but there are other options too.

The Three-Days-On/Four-Days-Off Routine

If studying every day is too much, follow the 15/30/15 Routine for three days per week, and take four days off. On your off days, spend just a few minutes reviewing everything from before, but you do not need to go any further at this stage in your course.

You will find this routine helpful if you are learning a difficult language, as your 'off' days will give you time to absorb and think about the information.

If you are having language lessons with a teacher or in a group, you may want to schedule those lessons for your 'off' days, and use them as a review of what you have been studying previously.

Once or Twice Per Week

When you get to an advanced level, you may find it helpful to study just once or twice per week. At this level, the vocabulary that you are learning is far more abstract, and your focus is on expressing yourself as idiomatically as possible like a native speaker. That means you may find it takes longer to remember new words, and you may be in need of more review time and more breaks.

With this rhythm, you will probably tend to study for full hours, rather than splitting your time up into smaller chunks. This is because you will be challenging yourself with longer, more complicated exercises, articles and writing tasks that require more of your concentration. On your 'off' days, you can re-read things, review and test yourself on the new vocabulary you've noted, and listen to podcasts and radio talk shows.

Forming Good Habits

By far the best way to use your time efficiently is to form good habits that you can rely on. That means that no matter what happens, it will feel more natural to make time for language learning than not.

The key to forming good habits is as much about your mindset as it is about anything else. In the next five steps, you will learn how to create new routines.

1. DREAM BIG, THINK SMALL

Believe that what you want to do is possible. If you are har-bouring doubts, these will limit your ability to achieve what you want. In other words, dream big. Imagine where you want to be, and focus on exactly how much you want it. This is your long-term goal.

To bridge the gap between where you want to be, and where you are at the moment, it's also crucial that you think about the steps you'll take to get there. This is where you need to think small. Set yourself learning quotas to fulfil each day and each week, then really focus on achieving these.

Your small steps should be manageable each day, and by doing them you motivate yourself to keep going and stick to your new routine. It is easy to get distracted by the bigger picture, but ultimately if you don't focus on the small steps first, your big dream will not get any closer.

2. BEHAVIOUR CHAINS

Instead of fighting against your existing routine, make use of it. Don't replace anything you do at the moment, instead just add extra chains to it that involve language learning. This will make sure not only that you schedule language learning in, but also that you are clear about what you should be doing, and when you should be doing it.

Let's imagine you have an existing behaviour chain that goes like this:

Get home from work –> Put kettle on –> Get changed –> Watch TV –> Cook –> Eat –> Watch TV –> Sleep

At any of these points (except between cooking and eating) you could add an extra chain that involves language learning and tell yourself: 'When I've got home from work, put the kettle on, and got changed, I will study for 30 minutes.'

This is a specific action point and fits within the framework of what you're doing already, so this is far more likely to work than if you just say 'I'm going to study every evening', which could leave you feeling stressed and distressed by the thought of suddenly cancelling all of the other things that make up your routine.

3. ELIMINATE EXCESSIVE OPTIONS

Making decisions takes up a lot of brain power. That distracts you from your short- and long-term goals and, before you know it, another week has gone by without you sitting down to study.

Identify all of the mundane aspects of your life and turn them into a routine that you no longer have to think about. Instead of spending hours each day thinking about what to eat for dinner that night, decide that on Mondays you eat fish, on Tuesdays pasta, on Wednesdays chicken and so on. Immediately you have freed up an enormous amount of thought space that you can use to focus on learning languages, and no longer have to plan trips to the supermarket and working out which ingredients you need to buy.

As President of the United States, Barack Obama famously only wore blue or grey suits. He said that not thinking about what to wear each day allowed him to focus on making the many more important decisions he faced.

4. PLAN THE PROCESS, NOT JUST THE OUTCOME

Fantasising excessively about the outcome of what you're doing can actually distract you from doing it in the first place. Yes, it's important to think about what that end goal might look like, but if you don't think about *how* you're going to get there then it will never get any closer.

Sit down and imagine exactly what you are going to be doing each day. Visualise yourself sitting with your books, talking to your teacher, making notes to videos on YouTube, and create a study plan along those lines. Then start implementing it.

5. ELIMINATE YOUR OBSTACLES

Think of every excuse you've ever come up with for missing a study day, or being behind on your goals. Work out what the obstacle has been on each occasion, and eliminate it.

Common problems can be not having a good space to work in, not being able to find a book, feeling tired, not doing homework and so on.

With each of these there are simple solutions: clear a space at home that you just use for language study, or pick a café or library you can go to instead. Keep your books somewhere you can always find them. Fit in your study time when you are not tired, and perhaps even find a different time of the day instead. And schedule your homework in using a Behaviour Chain so that you don't feel you have to miss class.

We all make up excuses for not staying true to our commitments, but ultimately we are the ones that suffer. Reduce the excuses and you'll reach your goals in no time.

The 'Less Is More' Principle

Rather than ploughing through your studies when you have a spare few hours, break up your study time and focus on achieving lots of small but efficient bursts. This is the thinking behind the 15/30/15 Routine.

Small bursts with regular breaks help to keep your brain fresh, your memory active, and your enthusiasm at its peak. If you sit down and study for hours, your brain will become overloaded with information, you will forget everything far quicker, and you will be far less likely to go back to studying the next day.

By doing less more frequently, you end up doing more in the longer term. The trick is to always take a break just as you really feel that you're enjoying what you're doing and making really good progress. That way, you always end your study sessions on a high, and never end them feeling tired or looking forward to doing something else.

By always having positive experiences of studying, you will find yourself constantly looking forward to getting back to it, and that you will naturally make the best use out of the time you allocate to studying.

The 'Two-Speed Study System'

Every exercise you do when learning a language will fall into one of two categories: active or passive. Some exercises require lots of thought and concentration, and can only be done in specially designated study slots. Others do not require your full attention but are vital in the longer term to making progress and making your active study time count.

If we use running as an analogy: you can either jog or sprint. Sprint training will get you running faster and gradually increase your stamina, but jogging will maintain your overall fitness and make sure that when you come to sprint training, you are still in shape. Finding the balance between these two modes is the key to becoming a good runner.

Generally, people who learn languages focus on the sprint but neglect the jog or the other way around. They put the time in for their active study, but forget about passive study, or spend hours listening to foreign songs they like but forget to ever open a grammar book.

Passive study is anything that involves contact with the language and an opportunity to be reminded of words and grammar that you already know, but without requiring any concentrated effort to get there. Watching a film with subtitles, having a chat with a friend, or just listening to audio are all excellent passive study activities that will bridge the gaps between your active study sessions.

Active study activities include grammar exercises, reading comprehensions, writing assignments, learning vocabulary and translations. All of these require concentration and dedication to complete them successfully.

Making Use of Your 'Dead Time'

Passive study activities are so useful for language learners because it's possible to do them when you couldn't be doing anything else. All of us in our routines have moments when we are technically busy, but our minds are free to run loose. You might be spending this time staring out the window, checking Facebook, or re-washing your hair. After reading this chapter, you will be filling this time with fun and useful language-learning activities.

Some of the most common instances of 'dead time' are: performing household chores, commuting, exercising, shopping, and relaxing. All of these present a golden opportunity to learn languages.

With a smartphone, you can take podcasts and live internet radio with you and listen along as you drive, sit on the bus, iron, cook, jog or go shopping. This gives you contact with the language that you otherwise would never have had, without preventing you from getting on with your daily life.

You may also think about replacing leisure activities with ones more to do with languages. Start watching more films in the language you're learning, even with subtitles, and you will gradually start to adjust more to the sound of the language, and even recognise words when you come to learn them later.

Listening to songs in a foreign language is one of the best ways to learn vocabulary (see Chapter 4). Provided that you can find music that you actually enjoy listening to, the rhythm, rhyme and repetition will all help you to learn words more easily without you even realising it.

When to Take Breaks

Taking breaks can be a powerful and useful way to improve your learning. Once you have got into a good routine and are making efficient use of your time, the idea of taking a week or two off learning might feel counter-productive. However, here are some reasons why it might be exactly what you need to keep everything going in the long term:

★ When you get back to learning you will feel refreshed and re-energised. This will avoid burnout in the longer term.
★ You will realise that you've remembered more than you thought you would. This is a sign of how well you've learned everything so far.
★ Devote some time to the other hobbies that you love. That way you'll feel your time is balanced and under control.

A natural opportunity to take a break is when a goal or milestone has been reached. You may then want to have a few weeks' rest before you start planning how to tackle the next stage of your learning.

Dealing with Sudden Changes to Routine

Things can always crop up that will throw you off course. Try not to get too frustrated if that means you end up taking an unplanned break from studying. Remember that you are human, and that learning a foreign language is something entirely humanly possible.

If you do end up in this situation, here are some ways to deal with it:

★ Learning things for the second time is far easier than the first time. Don't be discouraged if you feel you've gone backwards, just pick up the books and you'll find you remember it all in no time.

★ Don't be afraid to go back over chapters and topics you covered before your break. Chances are, you would have been due for some review anyway, so this is the perfect chance to directly face what you need to revise and relearn.

★ If you find your motivation dropping, turn back to the reasons you set out for why you wanted to learn this language at the end of Chapter 1. Those should be just as valid and comprehensive then as they are now.

HOW TO SPEAK ANY LANGUAGE FLUENTLY

Exercises

....

1. Take a weekly planner and mark up all of your time taken up by work and other commitments, leaving your free time. Schedule your study time in.

2. Identify the 'dead time' in your schedule and work out which moments you are definitely going to use for language study.

3. Write down every excuse you have ever given yourself for failing to do your language study for that day. Find ways to solve these problems and help make sure they never come up again.

4. Brainstorm a list of all the different possible activities you could be doing in your 'dead time', starting with the most relevant to your course and ending with the least relevant. Pick the ones you will start work on straightaway.

5. If you manage to make it through a whole week without missing a study slot, plan ways in which to reward yourself.

1. Person B's schedule is quite busy, yet he has cleared three slots in which he can commit to at least 30 minutes of Spanish study. These are immediately after he gets home, with a longer slot on Sunday afternoons.

	Mon	Tue	Wed	Thu	Fri	Sat	Sun
7.00							
8.00	Commute						
9.00	Work					Chores	
10.00						Amateur 5-a-side	
11.00							
12.00							Seeing family
13.00	Lunch Break						
14.00	Work					Watching football	
15.00							
16.00							STUDY
17.00							STUDY
18.00	Commute						
19.00	Gym	**STUDY**	Gym	**STUDY**	Pub	Pub	TV
20.00	Dinner						

2. Person B doesn't want commit to commit his lunch breaks to language study because he often needs to talk to his colleagues. His long commute in the mornings and evenings is the perfect time to read football news in Spanish or listen to some Spanish sports podcasts. He can also use his time at the gym to listen to audio or revise flashcards.

3.

Excuse	Solution
I got home late from work and half my study slot is gone.	Missing a few minutes here and there is not the end of the world. Besides, even just doing half your study slot is better than not doing anything at all. If you find this keeps happening, think about rescheduling.
My flatmate cleaned the front room and I have no idea where my books are.	Organisation is your top priority. Always know where your books are, and keep them in a safe place where they won't get lost.
The internet's down and I can't log in to Skype for my lesson.	Use the time. Do something from your textbook, write an email to your teacher with questions, spend 30 minutes writing about your day, or write a letter to your internet provider about how unhappy you are with their service!
I got injured playing football and it's hard for me to concentrate.	Do some activities that require less concentration. Watch a match on Spanish TV or a film with subtitles, or listen to the radio.
I'm tired and I just don't feel like it.	Everyone feels this way sometimes. But the feeling of guilt when you've let a whole day go to waste is worse. Look through your ten motivators from Chapter 1.

4.

Listen to slow news in Spanish

Listen to football on the radio

Listen to Spanish music

Watch Spanish films

Dead Time Activities

Change your phone's language to Spanish

Follow Sergio Ramos on Twitter

Watch kids' TV in Spanish

Revise flashcards

5. Every time he completes a week without missing a study session, Person B has decided to put some money in his 'Real Madrid Jar'. He's worked out that if he sticks to his commitments, after six months of study he'll have saved enough to afford a trip to Spain and watch his favourite team play.

HOW TO SPEAK ANY LANGUAGE FLUENTLY

CHAPTER 3

Learning with Teachers and Taking Courses

Learning a language by yourself can take you so far, but ultimately if you want to be able to speak it, you're going to have to practise it with someone else. Taking language lessons is the best way to do this.

Many of us actively avoid language lessons because of negative experiences at school, or perhaps because we think that we know our learning style best. However, with careful planning and the right attitude, language lessons can quickly become your most useful learning resource.

This chapter is all about making language lessons work for you.

Groups or One-to-One?

If you've decided to take lessons in the language you're learning, you'll be faced with a choice: join a group, or find a private teacher.

Both group and one-to-one lessons have advantages and disadvantages. They can also serve very different purposes, depending on your objectives and motivations. Here are some things to think about:

ONE-TO-ONE: ADVANTAGES

★ It's far easier to focus just on your learning style, needs and preferences

★ Lesson times are far more flexible

★ You make faster progress and speak much more

★ You set the pace and don't have to make allowances for other people

★ You don't have to be shy about making mistakes in front of others

ONE-TO-ONE: DISADVANTAGES

★ You may not get on with your teacher

★ The cost of private lessons is significantly higher

★ You can't compare your progress to your peers

★ One-to-one lessons require a lot more concentration and can be tiring

★ You can't learn from other people in your group

GROUPS: ADVANTAGES

★ These are *much* cheaper than private lessons

★ They are a great way to socialise and meet people with similar interests

★ Learning with other people can really boost your morale

★ You can learn from other people's mistakes and successes

★ If you're tired the spotlight is not constantly on you, as in a one-to-one lesson

GROUPS: DISADVANTAGES

★ Your progress is slower than with a private teacher

★ Lesson times are not flexible

★ There's a danger of learning other people's mistakes

★ You practise speaking mainly to other learners, not native speakers

★ Even within one group there can be a huge difference in ability and level

Where to Find Courses

If you live in a city, group language courses are easy to find if you know where to look.

See what your **local university** offers. Many universities run language classes open to the public as well as to students and staff. This is a great chance to get to use their excellent facilities and teaching expertise.

Beyond that, many **adult education centres** offer language courses too. These are often part-funded by local government, which means prices are kept low. Usually they offer evening classes, workshops on specific topics like pronunciation or writing, introductions to culture, and holiday crash-courses.

Your language may also be taught at a national **cultural centre**, part-funded by that country's government. These courses are usually of a very high standard and come with perks like being able to use the library, invitations to cultural events like film nights and exhibitions, and information about summer schools and courses you can take in the country itself.

There are a large number of **private language schools** that also offer courses. You may see these advertised in the local paper or on the internet. These might not come with all the perks of the others, but generally have a smaller, more personal set-up, which you may prefer.

DID YOU KNOW?

Some languages may also be taught at **churches, mosques, synagogues** and **community centres**, if you live in an area with a large expatriate community from those countries.

Make Groups Work for You

WHAT TO REMEMBER:

★ **Bring lots of patience**. You are sharing the classroom with other people who have different strengths and weaknesses to you.

★ **You're here to make new friends**. Getting on well with your peers will also make the whole learning experience a lot better.

★ **Learn from your peers**. Don't just listen to the teacher. The way other people in your group speak can be just as valuable a way for you to learn more.

Learning in a group is about the experience as well as the language you are learning. You should go there to have fun, and look forward to your lessons each week.

As an adult, this could be the first time you've stepped back into the classroom since school. That can bring back some interesting memories! Adult education is different to being at school, but some things will be familiar. Remember your teacher is just doing their job and at times might need your co-operation to help the class focus. At times you may feel infantilised, but this should be done with good humour and you should feel free to play along.

Listen carefully to how your classmates speak. Ask yourself: Could I have come up with that sentence by myself? Or: Are those words that I know or should I learn them? Keep a note of nice phrases or words you hear others using and revise them later.

Listen out for their mistakes, too. Ask yourself: Why are they making that mistake? Is there something in your first language that is 'interfering'? For example in English you say: 'I have gone to the shops', but in many other European languages you say: 'I *am* gone to the shops'.

Getting Ahead of the Class

Within one class there are often very different levels of ability. No matter how large the centre where you're taking your course is, compromises are often made and you might be put in a group where you don't feel you really belong.

There are different reasons why this might happen. You may have been learning the language longer than the rest of the group or be more familiar with a particular topic. Or you could be working harder than your classmates and making faster progress.

Whatever is going on, remember to remain patient. Keep the classroom environment a nice place for everyone. Make sure you always do as well as you can in your homework. Writing tasks in particular are the perfect opportunity to test your limits and make more progress, while getting feedback and corrections from a teacher.

Your teacher will be monitoring the various abilities in the group and will probably have noticed you are ahead. Stay on their side, and use time just after class to ask questions you don't think are relevant for the rest of the group. Your teacher may then suggest additional exercises you can do for more of a challenge.

This is a tricky issue, and possibly the main reason why people might opt for private teaching rather than a group course. However, remember that what this course is really offering you is a chance to practise and get exposure to the language you're learning regularly. Attending a course that isn't that challenging is still better than not having any lessons at all!

Falling Behind the Class

Perhaps worse than getting ahead is feeling you're getting behind. Sitting through a class where you understand almost nothing can be frustrating, especially if everybody else seems to be getting by with no problems. But don't worry, this isn't always as bad as it seems.

Firstly, congratulations. You are the luckiest person in the class, because you are going to learn the most. Leave each lesson with pages of notes, determined to come back next time with as much of it learned as possible. You also have the added advantage of being surrounded by other people who *have* learned this language well enough to impress you, and now you can model your own progress on their success.

HOW TO SPEAK ANY LANGUAGE FLUENTLY

> **Remember**: in a group environment everybody has something to contribute, and that includes you. You can always be a positive and productive member of the group and help to make it a healthy learning environment for everybody.

But if, as the weeks go by, it still feels like you've been put in too deep, don't worry. Level testing is not always precise, and it's possible there's been a mistake. Speak to your teacher and see if they agree that you might do better off in another group first. And remember, there are lots of different paths to the top.

Where to Find a Teacher

If you've decided one-to-one is the way to go, your next task will be finding a teacher. Many of the places you would look for group courses also offer private lessons. The challenge, though, is finding the right teacher.

Language teachers either work through a school or privately. You can find private teachers through classified ads, or on websites like iTalki.com, myngle.com and many others.

A **language school** can offer you flexibility. If one teacher can't make your preferred times and days, there are plenty more that can. Rates are all agreed far in advance and you will never pay your teacher directly. Your teacher is less likely to cancel lessons, and if they do, the school will arrange cover. Always ask what each school's policy on cancellations is.

A **private teacher** works for his or herself. It's very important to develop a good relationship with this person, as they are also their own secretary, accounts manager and curriculum designer. Rates may vary, but you can be sure that unlike in a school, the teacher will receive all what you're paying, which can raise their morale and enthusiasm.

Always ask to meet your teacher before booking a course. You will be spending a lot of time with this person, and so it is important that you get on and that you feel you can work with them.

Building the Perfect Relationship with Your Teacher: Five Steps

The relationship you will have with your language teacher will be defined by two key factors:

★ **Professionalism** – working with students like you is your teacher's full-time job. There's always work to do, and your teacher should make sure you do it.

★ **Money** – there is money on the table as you are paying for your teacher's time. Remember though, in education the customer might not *always* be right.

The best student-teacher relationships are when both people genuinely get on and share interests. Don't expect to click with them straight away, but after you've had a few lessons you will get to know each other, and be able to work better together.

KEY POINT

Many student-teacher relationships fail too early. It takes time for the teacher to adapt to your personal learning style and understand your motivations and goals. Even if things don't work out at first, try to complete at least 6 weeks of lessons before deciding whether to find a new teacher.

In many ways, having a good teacher is just as much about being a good student. Here are five steps to follow to make that happen:

1. COMMUNICATION

So your teacher can plan how to make the best use of your time together, always tell them as much detail as possible about:

★ Why you want to learn this language (see Chapter 1).
★ Where and how you've studied languages before, if at all (e.g. at school, private lessons, on your own, through the internet) and which course or textbooks you're familiar with.
★ What you like and dislike about learning languages.
★ What you can do in the language so far, and what you'd like to be able to do by the end of the course.

2. EXPECTATIONS

It's essential that you enter the relationship understanding *how* time with a teacher can benefit your language learning, and also what responsibilities you're left with. Remember:

★ Language lessons are one resource, but not the only resource. You will need to keep up regular independent study to really make progress.

★ Not all your lessons will be fun. You will cover topics that do and don't naturally interest you. Your teacher's job is also to encourage you to cover areas you're not naturally drawn to.

★ Your teacher will have their own style, and to some extent you will have to adjust to it.

3. ENGAGEMENT

Ideally, you want to become the student that your teacher really *wants* to help. Show them that you enjoy and appreciate their lessons in the following ways:

★ Pay attention to your body language. Smile and show your enthusiasm at all opportunities. This is especially important for Skype and other online lessons.

★ Always do the homework that your teacher sets. Often your next lesson may depend on completing the homework!

★ Ask as many questions as you can, both about things in class but also what you've learned from your solo study time.

★ Tell your teacher about other resources that you're using and ask for their opinions and recommendations.

4. FEEDBACK

Giving negative feedback to a teacher can be intimidating, but is often essential for securing your relationship. Just always remember:

★ Everybody likes hearing positive feedback when it's deserved.

- ★ Even if your teacher initially rejects the feedback, you will still have opened a dialogue that should eventually lead to improvements.
- ★ Giving feedback face-to-face can lead to fewer misunderstandings than by email.
- ★ Avoid making comparisons to previous teachers or learning experiences.

5. GOALS

Ultimately, you want to enter into this relationship with a clear idea of where you want to end up. Sit down with your teacher and agree on goals that you can set, and use these to measure your progress. If you're not meeting these goals, raise it with your teacher. Remember to make these objectives as clear as possible, such as:

- ★ Being able to read a specific text, or type of text e.g. a newspaper.
- ★ Completing a textbook.
- ★ Taking an exam/test.
- ★ Preparing for a trip abroad.

HOW LONG AND HOW OFTEN SHOULD EACH LESSON BE?

Try to always have more than one lesson per week, ideally two or three. This keeps everything fresh in your mind, and if you miss a homework day it won't be a whole week before you see the language again.

Normally lessons are sixty minutes each, but there is no fixed rule. If you're getting tired, try forty-five minutes instead. If you just want conversation, then thirty minutes is more than enough. By reducing the length of each lesson, you can probably afford to have lessons on more days of the week.

Taking lessons online makes shorter lessons more feasible for both parties, as there is no travel time involved.

Preparing for Your Lessons

Just as your teacher prepares for your lessons, you should too in order to get the most out of them. Remember, language lessons do not replace solo study time, but complement it. You should always be sticking to the study times you committed to in Chapter 2.

Specifically preparing for lessons should not take long, and counts as a useful activity for solo study time.

★ Always review what you covered in the previous lesson *at least* once. This includes both your notes and any material from the textbook.

★ Learn the ten most important words from the last lesson. If you have more than ten, ask your teacher which ones to focus on.

★ Come to each lesson with some questions to ask. These can be about language, or practical things like courses or resources your teacher can recommend.

★ Bring a vocab checklist to each lesson and aim to use all of it in conversation. Base this both on your words from the previous lesson, and new ones that you've come across in the meantime.

Hacking Homework

Doing homework may not be the most exciting thought in the world, but it is a vital part of the learning process. By doing it, you are helping yourself to get ahead.

Homework is a chance for you to build on whatever you've been covering with your teacher and continue learning out of class. It makes your time with your teacher go even further, and will make sure you're up-to-date and ready to make more progress in your next lesson.

Typically, there are a few types of task that you will be set. Here is how to get the most out of these:

1. WRITING TASKS

This is the most creative of homework tasks, where you can really push yourself. Always use a dictionary so you can be as ambitious as you can with your vocabulary. Don't worry about making mistakes. Your teacher will give you feedback, which is a chance to ask about anything that needs a clearer explanation. If anything, the more mistakes, the more opportunities to learn. After you have received your written work back, make sure you correct your mistakes and find time to rewrite it.

2. READING TASKS

If your teacher asks you to read a short text for homework, that almost always means you will talk about it in your next lesson. Make sure you read it! Always do so carefully and make sure you are comfortable with what it means, and 'how' it means that. Make notes on content, and look up words you don't know. Ideally re-read it several times. (See Chapter 8 for more on reading techniques.)

3. EXERCISES

If you've learned new grammar, your homework will be to practise and apply it. Normally this is done through exercises like 'Fill the gaps', 'Match the answers' or 'Translate these sentences'. The content of these exercises might not always seem completely relevant to you, but try to tolerate them as much as you can.

Here is one hack to make them work for you: Rewrite each sentence, practising the same grammar, but making them about you or someone you know. For example:

Q:	Meine Tante sitzt im Garten und trinkt Tee.
[Relevant version]:	Meine Tante sitzt **in der Kneipe** und trinkt **Bier**.

Your aunt probably doesn't sit in the garden and drink tea. She much prefers to sit in the pub and drink beer, and so that is what you should talk about in your homework instead.

Not only does talking about real people make the exercises more engaging, but you're also preparing sentences that one day you might actually need to say!

Online vs. Offline

Skype, Google Hangout, and other Video Chat applications make lessons possible with anybody, anywhere in the world. You don't have to travel, you're not restricted just to the teachers who live in your area, and you don't even have to worry about tidying the house before they come round.

The convenience of being able to open your computer at any moment and immediately be in the classroom is a powerful reason why many people prefer online lessons. They are also more affordable, and ideal if you like using YouTube videos and other Internet resources to study languages.

Programmes like Google Docs help to keep notes you can both access and edit simultaneously. This makes your lessons more organised and will also mean that you will never have to worry about losing notes or hand-outs.

However, there are some ways in which online interaction does fall short of meeting face-to-face meetings. With careful planning though, these can be overcome.

★ It's impossible to make direct eye-contact with someone over Skype, as looking at the webcam means looking away from the screen. Think about your body language and find other ways to show that you are engaged.

★ Make sure that you have a quiet place where you can sit uninterrupted for the duration of your lesson. Public spaces like cafés, bars or libraries are not advisable.

★ Internet reliability can vary and be disruptive. If you're at home, politely ask other members of your household if they can refrain from using the internet during your lesson to increase the quality. If the connection gets really bad, turn off video and just use voice until it sorts itself out.

★ In online lessons you are likely to write far less by hand (if at all), therefore discounting yourself from the benefit of developing muscle memory or being more creative in your assignments. If you like writing by hand, make notes with a pen and paper, and scan and email handwritten homework to your teacher.

Signs to Look Out For

With careful planning and an awareness of the issues that might crop up, you should have a great experience learning languages with a teacher. However, sometimes people just don't click, and if you've tried everything in this chapter and it's still not going well, it might be time to move on.

Try to anticipate this by looking out for these signs:

★ **You're stagnating**. Progress is not happening any longer and you no longer feel challenged.

★ **Feedback is ignored**. You've suggested changes you'd like to make to your lesson, but your teacher hasn't implemented them.

★ **Your goals feel further away**. Remember these? They should be getting closer with each week that passes, not sinking into the distance.

★ **You don't look forward to lessons**. They should always be enjoyable, even if they're hard.

If you do decide to stop lessons with your teacher, try to look positively at the experience and remember the many things you've learned from them – both about the language, and about the learning process itself.

Exercises

1. Write down all of the negative experiences you have had from working with a teacher in the past. Try to come up with ways to overcome those problems this time round.

2. Research all of the courses and private teachers that are available to you both online and in your area. Rate them all on the basis of:

   a   Ease of access
   b   Reputation
   c   Response to your enquiry
   d   Cost

3. Take a trial lesson online via Skype and compare your experience to learning with a teacher face-to-face.

4. Think of some ways to enhance your homework tasks and get more out of those activities. Even just spending 25 per cent more time on each task could give you fresh ideas.

5. After the first month of taking lessons, list all of the positives and negatives that you have noticed so far. Find a way to give constructive feedback to your teacher and suggest ways to make improvements.

Model Answers: Person C

1.

Negative experiences	Ways to overcome them
Teacher corrected her all the time.	Ask the teacher to write down mistakes for you to correct yourself.
Spent all her time listening to other people but never spoke herself.	Book private lessons with a teacher online or offline for 30–45 minutes per week.
Lessons were about things she wasn't interested in.	Tell your teacher about your interests and motivations. Send them links to articles or blog posts that you find interesting and ask if you can work on things like that.
Teacher clearly didn't plan lessons and they felt unstructured.	In future, book a trial lesson first and see if you like your teacher's style. Ask your teacher about structure and lesson aims.
Teacher moved too fast and didn't leave time to repeat or revise things.	Ask your teacher about the structure of the whole course. Ask when there'll be revision and repetition, and about mid-course tests. Ask which textbooks the teacher uses, and do some revision from that in your private study time.

2. **a.** Course option 1:

Good reputation and very close to work. Responded to by receptionist who sounded like she dealt with enquiries every day. Group course about £235 per term. Includes access to library.

b. Course option 2:

Good reputation but mixed reviews on Google. Easily accessible from work. Nice receptionist who explained all the options, including private lessons. £150 for two-week course. No extras.

c. Course option 3:

Hard to find information online but offering a wide range of languages. Put through to a call centre when called. £225 for a 10-week group course.

3. Offline experience:

I had my first lesson with Andrea today. Andrea was nice and we had a basic conversation. He asked me what I do, if I liked it, how long I'd been living in London and the usual things. He wrote down the words I needed. We read a bit from a textbook and did some exercises. He's set me the rest for homework. Andrea was really nice and encouraging and I'm happy to be working with him. I found the lesson a lot more tiring than I'd expected, though, especially after a long day at work, and even though we'd booked an hour I felt just about done after 35 minutes. When I got home, I just collapsed in front of the TV. It was fun though, and I'm looking forward to next week!

Online experience:

I got home from work today and went straight to my laptop to turn on Skype and have my first online lesson with Maria. It was quite strange at first, and we spent the first five minutes asking 'Can you hear me?', but then it felt like any other lesson. We had some basic conversation, and Maria showed me a presentation she'd made about her town. I read bits out and did some comprehension exercises and grammar. Again, I was pretty exhausted just after half-way through, so next time I think I'll just book 45 minutes instead – as I wasn't travelling to my lesson, 45 minutes still felt worthwhile. Maria suggested we schedule a 25–30-minute chat each week during my lunch break. I can sit somewhere at work with my laptop and sandwich and do that! I'm amazed at how natural the whole thing felt and I'm looking forward to my lesson with Maria next week.

4. • Rewrite homework exercises to make them more relevant to me or someone that I know.
   • Use a dictionary to write 'what-happens-next?' sentences after each question, e.g.:

   Question sentence: *Ai miei genitori piace andare in vacanza in Toscana.*
   My parents like to go on holiday in Tuscany.

What Happens Next: *A loro piace bere molto vino rosso. A loro piace portare a casa molte bottiglie nella loro valigia. Sono bravi a nasconderle alla dogana dell'aeroporto.*

They like to drink lots of red wine. They like to bring many bottles home in their suitcase. They are good at hiding them from Customs at the airport.

- Create flashcards or Memrise lists for all new vocabulary. Find pictures on Google Images/Instagram for them, and review them regularly.
- Write five more sentences for each grammar exercise, practising the same thing.
- Think of three questions to ask your teacher each week, based on your homework and any extra study.

5.

Positives: — Maria always smiles and cheers me up, even if I've had a long day!

— Maria loves it if I ask lots of 'irrelevant' questions and is never afraid to diverge from the lesson plan if it's interesting.

— Maria sets good amounts of homework. We correct it together and I have to understand why something is wrong before we move on.

— I'm learning lots of useful phrases that I can imagine using with Italians!

Negatives: — Maria is speaking a lot of English to me. That was helpful at first, but I'd like to hear more Italian now.

— We start and end five minutes late. It's not a huge problem, but I'd like to stick to the schedule.

— Maria is always making jokes about England. At first I laughed, but it's starting to get tiring.

Feedback: Tell Maria how much I enjoy the lessons and I want to continue. Ask her to speak more Italian, even if I don't always understand. Ask her to just talk about Italy, because that's what I'm interested in. Tell her that I want to end lessons on time.

CHAPTER 4

Learning Vocabulary

When you think about learning vocabulary, you will probably think of one thing: vocab tests. You may remember trying to cram as many words into your head before school, only to write them all down in the test and forget them moments later.

Without any context, memorising lists of vocabulary to be tested on can be frustrating and extremely counterproductive. As an adult learner, these no longer have to be a part of the way you learn languages.

Why Learn Vocabulary?

In this chapter, we will look at ten top techniques for learning new words that you can start using right away.

But first of all, let's remind ourselves why we should be learning vocabulary in the first place. Here are three very important reasons:

1. LANGUAGES ARE MADE OF WORDS

The more words that you know, the more things you can talk about. Grammar, pronunciation, reading and writing are also important, but ultimately without a decent-sized vocabulary you will find yourself restricted in what you can talk about in your new language.

2. IT CAN BE ENOUGH TO COMMUNICATE JUST WITH VOCABULARY

If you gesticulate and sound urgent enough, you can almost express yourself without any grammar at all. For example, if you've been bitten by a dog and need to tell someone, all you need to do is wave frantically and shout 'Dog bite hand!', and someone will get the message.

3. BROADER VOCABULARY BROADENS YOUR HORIZONS

One of the easy traps to fall into when learning a new language is complacency. It is easy to get comfortable with only talking about specific topics, never really branching out, and finding yourself in a bit of a rut. But if you keep learning new vocabulary, that is a way to break out of that pattern and start talking about more and more complex topics, while making sure that your progress doesn't stall.

How 'Actively' Should You Be Studying Vocabulary?

Learning vocabulary is important, but as with all things a balance needs to be struck in order to avoid either over-focusing on it, or not focusing on it enough. If you concentrate too much on learning lists of words, you may find this becomes as counterproductive as not learning any at all.

Here are some things to think about that should help you to establish whether or not you should be making vocabulary your key focus, or instead allowing it to sink in gradually as you make your way through your course.

WHY MAKE A SPECIAL EFFORT:

★ Actively learning vocabulary means you can be **thorough** in your approach. You are less likely to have **vocabulary gaps** as you move forward, meaning that you effectively will have learned the language better.

★ Learning vocabulary is **great exercise for the brain**. Even if you just spend ten minutes on it at a time, that is as good as doing a crossword or Sudoku puzzle a day. It forces you to be creative and to think laterally, which allows you to learn more.

★ Learning new words gives you a huge **confidence boost**, as you gradually feel yourself more and more able to take on all sorts of situations and handle them in the language you're learning.

WHY LET IT SINK IN GRADUALLY:

★ It is not helpful to sit and learn thousands of words that in the end **you might never need to use**. Lists are impersonal and don't directly relate to your needs and goals in the language you're learning.

★ Everything should be about **improving your speaking**. By learning words in isolation from a list, you don't see how they fit into a phrase or sentence that you might one day use. Knowing what a word means in theory does not guarantee that you will spontaneously be able to use it.

Ultimately, how much emphasis you put on learning vocabulary will come down to your personal preferences and needs. However, you will certainly find it hard to learn a language without some degree of learning vocabulary. Even just reviewing your notes once a week and reminding yourself of the new words you've been writing down will certainly help you to sustain your momentum.

If the idea of learning words still leaves you feeling unexcited, then you probably haven't yet found the method that really works for you. Learning a new language really is a very personal process, and certainly to begin with, a lot of your time will be spent experimenting and trying to work out what exactly suits you best.

That is precisely what we will discuss now. Which *type* of language learner do you think you are?

Understanding Your 'Learning Type'

The simplest way to understand different learning types is to break them down into three distinct categories: **Visual**, **Auditory** and **Kinaesthetic**. Note that it's rare for somebody to identify exclusively with just one of these three categories. Most people tend to feel that they are a mixture of these different strengths and preferences, and so bear that in mind when considering how this fits you. Nearly everybody will identify with two of these different categories, and some may even see in themselves aspects of all three.

Once you've read through these descriptions, if you're still unsure as to which category you fit into the best, there are many free tests you can find through Google that will help you to decide.

VISUAL LEARNERS

You remember best the things that you've seen. You can easily recall images such as pictures, diagrams, and video clips, and find that different colours and fonts are something that stick in your mind. At school you found it easiest to remember what the teacher wrote up on the board, or when your textbook used lots of pictures and diagrams to break up the text. You may find it easy to remember faces, but struggle to recall people's names. You typically have a vivid imagination, and tend to really use facial expressions to show your emotions.

AUDITORY LEARNERS

You remember best the things that you've heard. You can easily recall the spoken word in conversations, podcasts, radio shows, songs and anywhere in which there is speech. You'll find that pitch, volume and accent are some of things that really stick in your mind. You can also learn something by listening to yourself saying it. At school while the teacher was talking you would find yourself looking down at your desk and really focusing on what they were saying. You may find it easy to remember names, but hard to remember faces. At meetings you're probably not taking any notes or finding that you need to refer back to them to remember what was being said, as you simply retain better what you've heard.

KINAESTHETIC LEARNERS

You remember best not what people have said or look like, but what they've done. You remember places and actions and think about where you were and what you were doing when you found out a piece of information. At school you liked it when activities involved standing up, moving around, and rearranging things around the room. You learned the most on field trips, when you got to see the practical side of what you spent your time learning in the classroom. You typically learn by imitation and practice, and in your earlier life may have experienced difficulty learning to read. More often than not, kinaesthetic learners are active and athletic, and may be misunderstood as being slow if information is not presented to them in their particular style.

Learning According to Your Style: Ten Techniques

We're now going to look at ten different techniques for learning vocabulary. These are marked **V.**, **A.** or **K.** to show which learning styles they will appeal to most. Try as many of these out as you can, and see which ones you like the best.

1. LISTS – V. K.

This is one of the simplest and most 'traditional' methods of learning new vocabulary. Write out lists of new words that you come across, with the original on one side and the translation on the other. When you want to test yourself, you can cover the other side of the sheet of paper so you only see one language at a time. Note that testing yourself from your language into the target language is significantly more challenging than from the target language into yours, and so being able to do this should be seen as a sign that a word is well and truly learned.

The Pros: This method's strength lies in its simplicity. It also allows you to keep a note of new vocabulary alongside whatever other activity you're done, so long as you have a pen and paper to hand. **Visual learners** will enjoy seeing words written down and those with photographic memories will be able to recall the image of the page. **Kinaesthetic learners** will enjoy writing and moving the page around. **All learners** will notice that writing words out by hand increases their chances of learning by muscle memory, in other words physically remembering how they wrote the words out.

The Cons: Lists are not the most exciting way to learn vocabulary in the world. They can also get lost and tattered, and if you're learning a language with a different script you may struggle at first to perfect your handwriting. As with all techniques, they are best used in conjunction with others.

2. FLASHCARDS – V. K.

Instead of writing all your new words down on a single piece of paper, get a deck of note cards from a stationery shop and write each word out on a different card, with the translation on the back. Test yourself on one side, before checking the other. You'll find that some cards will be easier to remember, while others will be more difficult. Set the more difficult ones aside, and remember to spend more time on them. You could also get a set of envelopes to keep different flashcards in, and order them according to words you know well to the ones that you barely recognise, placing others in between. As you get words right or wrong, move them up or down into a different envelope, and remember to review them all regularly.

The Pros: Many people swear by flashcards, especially those with **visual** and **kinaesthetic** learning preferences. There is lots of room for creativity, such as using different colours and stickers, and you can also include as much or as little information about the grammar of a word as you like. Reviewing flashcards is perfect for **kinaesthetic learners** who can turn them over and see them in different places.

The Cons: After a while you may find that you have gathered an enormous number of these, and so it is no longer practical to review them as regularly as you once could. You also can't carry around large packages of flashcards everywhere, which becomes inconvenient. If you like flashcards though, these problems can partly be solved with new apps and technology like Anki and Memrise (see Method 4: Spaced Repetition Software), which allow you to store flashcards digitally on your phone or tablet.

3. LEARNING BY ROTE – A. (K.)

Rather than writing down a list, when you learn by rote you instead recite and memorise it. This is often used for learning verb conjugations and noun declensions (see Chapter 5), but can help you learn vocabulary too.

The Pros: Many people feel instinctively unsure about this method because it may bring back memories of having to do this at school in unison with your whole class. Nevertheless, for **auditory learners** this can be an extremely useful activity, as it allows them to hear the words that they are trying to learn, as opposed to just seeing them written down.

The Cons: The biggest challenge for this method is how to convert what is learned into language that can be used spontaneously, without having to recycle through memorised chants. With enough speaking practice this is possible, but it means scheduling that in is even more important than before.

4. SPACED REPETITION SOFTWARE – V. (K. A.)

Spaced Repetition Software (or S.R.S.) are apps and websites that calculate how often you need to see something in order to remember it. They work by sending you reminders that it is time to study, and work like electronic flashcards. Many of them also use plenty of 'gamification', which aims to distract you from the fact that you are learning with games, points and scoreboards where you can compare your progress to your friends. These are usually free, and can be an excellent way to manage your learning.

The Pros: **Visual learners** especially benefit from the presentation of these flashcards, which are often very colourful. Memrise is one of the largest S.R.S. systems for vocabulary learning, and is popular because it allows you to upload your own photos and create memes to go with your new words, creating strong visual associations. **Kinaesthetic learners** will appreciate typing up flashcards, and sometimes there are also audio recordings that are available for **auditory learners**.

The Cons: The downside to these is that they require you to be on your computer, phone or tablet, which means that a world of distractions is only just a click away. People who don't like constantly using technology may find that to be a problem. However, the carefully calculated intervals at which you should be studying are invaluable to **any language learner**. If you stick to them, you will notice a big improvement.

NOTABLE S.R.S. APPS/WEBSITES:

★ **Memrise** (www.memrise.com) for learning vocabulary. Many textbooks and courses also have their vocabulary uploaded here for your convenience.

★ **Anki** (www.anki.com) are like flashcards you can customise and keep on your phone, cutting out the paper problem.

★ **Duolingo** (www.duolingo.com) offers to teach you an entire language by translating short and simple sentences that gradually get harder.

5. MEMORISATION – A. V. (K.)

For this method all you have to do is memorise short passages in the language you're learning. These can be stories, poems or even dialogues. At first you will need to put some time in to learn these off by heart, but then it will quickly pay off. Not only will you be learning new words, but you'll also be learning whole sentences and phrases in which you can use them.

The Pros: **Visual learners** will enjoy memorising from the page, while **auditory learners** will find reciting them to be what helps them learn. **Kinaesthetic learners** can customise this to their needs by using actions, or moving around the room as they recite the passages.

The Cons: You may struggle to find short texts that use the vocabulary you want to learn, but you can solve this simply by writing your own. This allows you to be creative, and also use the extremely powerful tool of **context** to learn vocabulary, as we will see later in this chapter. Try to have your texts checked by a native speaker to avoid learning mistakes.

6. MUSIC – A.

Listening to music can be one of the most effective ways of learning new words. Music is catchy, and even those of us who are not natural **auditory learners** are more likely to remember a song than ordinary speech. This is helped by the fact that words are sung in time to a rhythm, and in many cases also rhyme with each other.

The Pros: Even if you don't understand songs when you first hear them, if you like them then it can be a good idea to keep listening. You may end up hearing a word so many times without realising it that when you eventually come to learn what it means, it's already fixed in your memory!

The Cons: The challenge can be finding songs with lyrics that are relevant, as this is not always possible. However, as many songs are about love and feelings, you can be sure that you will eventually become very familiar with this kind of vocabulary the more you listen to music.

7. LISTEN ON THE MOVE – K. A. (V.)

There's no reason why your language study should be confined to just one place. You can make use of all the moments you've got by listening to vocab lists and dialogues from your textbook while you're on the move too. Simply keep the files on your smartphone, MP3 player or tablet and listen through earphones next time you go for a walk, take the bus, or play them through the audio system in your car.

The Pros: This is the perfect activity for **kinaesthetic learners with auditory tendencies**. What's particularly useful about this method is that you will start to build associations between the new words you're learning, and the place where you first heard them.

The Cons: What you are doing while listening to your language-learning material may not always allow you to fully concentrate on the language. This means this is not always the most efficient way of learning vocabulary, but arguably you are still fitting it in at a time when you otherwise would not be doing any learning at all.

8. PUT STICKERS AROUND THE HOUSE – K. V.

If you're trying to learn a new set of vocabulary, try writing words on Post-it notes and stick them around the house in places you know you'll look at. For example, you might have one on the fridge, one on a window, on the back of the door and so on. Here the idea is that you will naturally look at these places at intervals, and eventually will start to remember them.

The Pros: Visualising and memorising the Post-it notes is great for **visual learners**, and the spatial associations of putting them in different places makes this a great activity for **kinaesthetic learners** too. When trying to remember a specific word, in your mind you can try to walk back to the different places around your home where you have put stickers which will help you to recall the word more easily.

The Cons: Make sure you remember to keep updating your stickers with new vocabulary that is still relevant to what you are trying to learn. However, you will find that you still have to make a conscious effort to read the Post-it notes each time you pass them for them to really sink in. Otherwise they may just fade in as part of the furniture.

TOP TIP: MIX THINGS UP

A variation on this is to take vocabulary lists with you when you leave the house and try to find the objects that you are learning. This really appeals to visual learners, and can be especially useful when learning vocabulary for topics like the town, fruit and vegetables, and so on. Alternatively, leave the lists at home and look around, trying to see if you can name things that you can see. If you can't, make a note and look it up when you get home.

9. STORYTELLING – V. A. K.

If you are faced with a set of vocabulary that you need to learn, one of the best ways to make it memorable is to inject some life into it by turning it into a story. You can either write this down or say it to your teacher or language partner. Simply go through the vocabulary and try to use one word in each sentence. Don't worry if it's not always coherent, sometimes the weirder a story is the easier it is to remember!

The Pros: This is something that can appeal to creative people, no matter what their learning preferences are. **Kinaesthetic** and **auditory** learners will prefer to tell their stories aloud with lots of actions, while **visual** learners will prefer to write them down.

The Cons: If you are not a naturally creative person in this sense, you may struggle slightly more with this task. You can overcome this by telling a story that you already know, or recounting anecdotes about your day instead, trying as much as possible to stick to the list of target vocabulary that you have.

10. MNEMONICS – V. A. K.

Mnemonics are a way to learn new words based on words you already know and what they remind you of. Try telling yourself a little story about each word to make it memorable, and depending on whether you are more visual, auditory or kinaesthetic you will want to play up its visual, sound or action associations each time.

The Pros: The key thing with mnemonics is that they should always be very personal to you. It's rare for you to be able to learn from other people's mnemonics. This is about how your brain works, and the connotations that a word might conjure up for you. Try to make your mnemonics as vivid and as graphic as possible – after all, you don't have to share them with anyone!

The Cons: You may end up remembering the mnemonic, but not the word! This is something that you can overcome with time, especially if you continue to have regular contact with the language and keep putting yourself in a position where you need to recall the words in context, not just as one-offs.

Here are some examples of mnemonics for words in Hungarian, a language totally unrelated to most European languages which can be a huge challenge to learn vocabulary for:

Hungarian	English	Mnemonic
titok	secret	Secretly, people thought Tito was O.K.
víz	water	The word 'water' starts with two 'V's
komóly	serious	Hungarians are serious about their comb oil.
bátya	older brother	Your older brother will bat ya.

Being able to create really memorable mnemonics is a skill that takes time to develop. Experiment with this as much as possible to see what works. The website Memrise is an excellent tool for seeing mnemonics other people have come up with, and also trying to come up with your own.

The Power of Context

Wherever possible, it's always best to learn a new word in its natural context. That means thinking about where you first came across it, and when you would use it. Memorise a short phrase with a word in it rather than just the word on its own. This helps to keep the meaning of a word closely associated with its use.

Ask anybody who has visited Berlin and used the U-Bahn if they learned any German during their stay. Almost certainly, they will tell you that one of the words they learned was 'Ausgang'. Every time they left a metro station, a shop, a restaurant, or any building they will have seen this word. They will have started to look for it in order to work out how to leave wherever they were. It will have become easy for them to remember this word, as they will have seen it everywhere, and they will have no doubt in their minds as to what it means, because every time they saw it in the **context** of leaving.

Learning words in their natural context helps to keep them **fresh** and **spontaneous** once you have learned them. It won't be hard for you to recall them when you need them, as the context of every time that you need to remember a word will automatically remind you of it.

> **TOP TIP: CREATE CONTEXT**
> Have conversations on specific topics, read articles about them and watch and listen to programmes about them as much as you can. That way when you come across new words it will be **easier to guess what they mean**, and also **easier to remember** them in the long term, as you will remember generally what was being said at the time.

Learn by Using

One of the most memorable ways of learning new words is to use them. Once you start encountering new vocabulary in different contexts and from different sources, you will soon find it much easier to remember words and you will no longer need to rely on mnemonics or other learning aides.

Your lessons with your teacher are one of the best opportunities to start doing this. Prepare vocabulary 'checklists' based on the words you are learning that week, and try to use each word at least once over the course of your lesson. You can also do this for language exchanges, or just for casual conversations if you are spending time in an immersed environment.

When you come across a word that you don't know – either in a lesson, a conversation, or just something you see one day – always try to ask what that word means. If you can find out there and then, you will develop a powerful link to that word as you will have learned it in its natural context.

Choosing and Prioritising Vocabulary

The biggest potential risk of actively trying to learn lots of vocabulary is that you end up wasting time learning words that realistically you will never use. This means that you will not see the results from all the time you're putting into learning, which will lead to your progress slowing, and your motivation dropping.

As a solution to this, simply don't learn those useless words at all! Instead, always learn the words that directly relate to your situation, and prioritise the ones that you know you will have to use.

For each vocabulary topic that you cover (e.g. the house, work, hobbies, the environment) plan out what you would like to say about each. You can even write out mind-maps of all the conversations you can potentially see yourself having, and work out which words you need to learn in order to have them.

For example, if you come from a very small family then learning all of the different words for relatives (e.g. younger brother, older brother, step-sister, second cousin and so on) is not your priority. Instead, you need words that *do* describe your situation, like 'only child' or 'I come from a small family'.

Think of this like your core set of key vocabulary. Once you've mastered that, you can then move on to more distant things that describe other people's situations, such as 'I am an only child, but my wife has two older brothers and a sister.'

Exercises

1. Experiment with all of the different vocabulary learning exercises from the last chapter and work out whether you prefer visual, auditory or kinaesthetic activities.

2. Take a recent list of vocabulary and come up with convincing mnemonics for at least ten words. After a few days, see which words you still remember and which words you don't. How decisive was the mnemonic you came up with in making these words memorable or not for you?

3. Aim to have at least one vocabulary-related study session every day for a week and see how much more memorable that makes the words in the long term. Increase or decrease the frequency with which you do this accordingly.

4. Choose an important vocabulary topic and brainstorm the most important words you think you'd need to be able to talk about it. Compare the differences in how easy or hard it is to remember this list than a general list given to you by your teacher or taken from your textbook.

5. Keep a notebook in which you write down every time you find yourself searching for a word that you don't know. Note how this gradually decreases as your course progresses and you find yourself learning more and more.

Model Answers: Person D

1. Person D is loves music. Vocabulary lists didn't work for him, and flashcards were not much better. He learnt best to anything auditory and kinaesthetic. He sang all his Russian vocabulary while he drove to work or did chores.

2.

Russian	English	Mnemonic
яблоко [yábloko]	apple	Put an apple in your mouth and *you-block-'er*.
апельсин [apelsín]	orange	An *apple* who's *sin*ned is an orange.
виноград [vinográd]	grape	In the wine town *Vinograd*, everyone eats grapes.
персик [pérsik]	peach	If you eat a *pear* and are *sick* you've got a peach.
клубника [klubníka]	strawberry	Strawberries are so cool they always go clubbing.
арбуз [arbúz]	watermelon	A watermelon is the same size as *our bus*.
малина [malína]	raspberry	Russian raspberries are evil, *malign* fruits.

3. Person D used his drive to work to focus on vocabulary and sing vocabulary songs. He also made up new ones. Russian vocabulary is very different to English, so he worried about not remembering words. But every morning he proved that he knew lots of words and was learning more all the time. In the evenings he focused on grammar, so he had all his bases covered.

4.

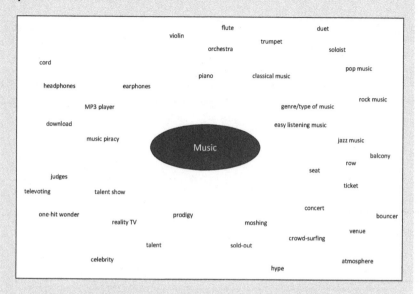

5. Person D wrote down words he couldn't think of during his language course and revised them every week. Eventually, he found he knew most of the words he needed to describe everyday topics. He then stretched himself by thinking of less common topics for which he needed much more vocabulary.

CHAPTER 5

Grasping Grammar

Grammar is what holds language together. Think of it as the glue, or if you prefer, the cement that holds together the bricks of vocabulary. As we saw previously, you can make yourself understood in a language without grammar. But making yourself understood is a long way off from really speaking a new language.

Unfortunately, people will probably not pick up on it when you flawlessly use perfect grammar. People will compliment your accent or be impressed if you can keep up with a conversation between native speakers, but efforts to learn grammar largely go unnoticed. That is because native speakers are rarely aware of the great challenge their language's grammar can present to the learner.

Ironically, you will attract attention if you keep making mistakes though. These may even tarnish your image. People love to hear foreign accents in their own language, but mistakes in grammar can really grate on the ear and are harder to overlook.

The good news is that grammar is finite, unlike almost everything else about learning a language. You'll forever be learning new words and expressions, but with grammar there is a finishing line.

But to get there, there are a few hurdles to clear first.

Why a Spade Isn't Just Called a Spade

Grammar tends to present language learners with two problems. Firstly, they must try to understand the grammar, and secondly they must try to understand the language used to explain the grammar.

Grammar jargon is intimidating, especially if you've never had much contact with it before. In some countries, such as many in the English-speaking world, grammar is not really taught in any detail in schools, which means that learning a foreign language is the first time that many people really come face-to-face with it.

Fortunately, all that jargon is doing is describing things you already know and say in your own language naturally. In other words, you already know everything about grammar. You just don't know that you know it yet.

It is very worthwhile to familiarise yourself with grammar terms at an early stage. Not only will this serve you for the language you're learning now, but will also be a great help to learn any further languages in the future. It is extremely useful to be able to see the similarities and the differences between different languages' grammars, as many concepts are directly transferable or very similar.

Common Terms Explained

This list is far from exhaustive, but will give you a great head start for studying grammar in any language.

ADJECTIVE

An adjective is a word that describes a **noun**.

For example: The sky is blue.

Unlike in English, in many languages it is important to change the endings of adjectives to match the nouns that they are describing, e.g. if it is plural, masculine, feminine etc. (see **gender**). This is called **adjectival agreement**.

ARTICLE (DEFINITE/INDEFINITE)

This is either the word 'the' (definite article) or 'a/an' (indefinite article). Some languages use the word 'the' more often than in English, while others don't use it at all. In some languages the word for 'a' or 'an' is the same as the word 'one'.

CASES

Cases are when a word changes slightly in order to express information about its role in a sentence. Languages like French, Spanish, Italian and Portuguese do not have cases. German, Russian, Greek, Polish and most Eastern European languages do.

For example: [German]

der Bruder — the brother (subject/ **nominative** case)

de**s** Bruder**s** — of the brother (**genitive** case)

This very slight change of adding the letter 's' and swapping 'r' for 's' in the definite article means you don't need to add the word 'of', unlike in English. The **genitive** case naturally implies the word 'of' without needing to spell it out.

Different languages can have different numbers of cases, and each case can do very different things. Approach each case with patience, and through regular practice you will eventually forget what life was like before you learned how to use them!

CLAUSE

A clause is like a phrase that constitutes the smallest grammatical part of a sentence that contains a complete proposition. In other words, clauses do not have to be part of a sentence. They can exist as sentences in their own right, but get added to larger sentences to make more complex and intricate points.

For example: 'I invited her to the cinema, but she didn't want to come.'

This sentence is made up of two mini-sentences, or clauses:

1. 'I invited her to the cinema.'
2. 'She didn't want to come.'

Some languages like German and Russian require you to separate clauses by always putting a comma [,] between them.

A **relative** or **subordinate** clause is more dependent on the **main** clause. Again, it could exist on its own, but makes more sense within the context of the **main** clause.

For example: "After I'd studied German, I decided to visit Berlin."
         [Subordinate]   **[Main]**

"The man | who said hello to me | had brown hair."
[Main]   **[Relative]**   **[Main continued]**

CONJUGATION

Conjugation is when a verb changes in order to reflect who is doing the action. In many languages, this usually happens at the *end* of the verb, although in some languages this may happen at the beginning or in the middle instead. English verbs have almost no conjugation, except for the 'he/she/it' form in the present tense, which makes this an unfamiliar concept to many learners. With regular practice, though, conjugation in any language is very easy to get used to.

The table below compares the verb 'to speak' in English with its Spanish equivalent. The conjugation of the verb is underlined.

Who?	English	Spanish
I	speak	hablo
you (singular)	speak	hablas
he/she/it	speaks	habla
we	speak	hablamos
you (plural)	speak	habláis
they	speak	hablan

As you can see, in Spanish the verb conjugates differently for every person. In English, the verb only conjugates for 'he/she/it', when it gains an '-s'.

Conjugation can also refer to different 'patterns' of verbs within a language. Unless they are irregular, all verbs will fit into a specific pattern or conjugation. All of the endings will be the same for all verbs in that conjugation.

In Spanish, there are three different conjugations. Their different endings are underlined in the table below:

Who?		1st Conjugation (-ar) hablar (to speak)	2nd Conjugation (-er) comer (to eat)	3rd Conjugation (-ir) vivir (to live)
I	yo	habl<u>o</u>	com<u>o</u>	viv<u>o</u>
you	tú	habl<u>as</u>	com<u>es</u>	viv<u>es</u>
he/she/it	él/ella	habl<u>a</u>	com<u>e</u>	viv<u>e</u>
we	nosotros	habl<u>amos</u>	com<u>emos</u>	viv<u>imos</u>
you (pl.)	vosotros	habl<u>áis</u>	com<u>éis</u>	viv<u>ís</u>
they	ellos/ellas	habl<u>an</u>	com<u>en</u>	viv<u>en</u>

As you can see, there are some slight differences between the three conjugations, which you will have to memorise. But once you have learned these, you will be able to use any verb in the whole of the Spanish language.

CONJUNCTION

Conjunctions are words that hold clauses, words and sentences together. You can think of them like 'glue' words.

There are three main categories:

1. **Co-ordinating** conjunctions, which either join or contrast ideas.

    For example: and, but, for, nor, or, so, yet

2. **Subordinating** conjunctions, which are used to introduce **subordinate clauses**.

    For example: while, because, even if, although, as soon as, after

3. **Correlative** conjunctions, which link two equal parts of a sentence.

    For example: either ... or ..., both ... and ..., neither ... nor ...

HOW TO SPEAK ANY LANGUAGE FLUENTLY

GENDER

Many languages divide words up into two or three genders. All words must be referred to as 'he', 'she' or 'it' accordingly.

Some languages have clear rules that can help you determine a word's gender, such as in Spanish where words ending in 'a' are usually feminine while words ending in 'o' are usually masculine. Other languages can be harder to predict and you must simply learn each word with its gender.

Often there is a direct correlation between a noun's gender and what it refers to, such as the word 'father' being masculine and 'mother' being feminine in French, but unfortunately this is not always as clear-cut and can never be presumed to be the case. Generally speaking, in languages that are all part of the same linguistic sub-family – such as French, Romanian, Italian, Catalan, Portuguese, and Spanish, which all derive directly from Latin – words tend to have the same gender, or at least greatly overlap. But again there are plenty of exceptions which mean that this cannot be always presumed.

For example:

Masculine	Translation	Feminine	Translation
le père	the father	la mère	the mother
le garçon	the boy	la fille	the girl
le soleil	the sun	la table	the table
le ciel	the sky	la neige	the snow
le poisson	the fish	la chaise	the chair

NOUN

A noun is a word that refers to a thing, an object, a person, a place or idea. A noun is a name for something.

For example: table, chair, lamppost, window, sun, feeling
but not: ~~realise, happy, shine, express~~

In most languages, **proper nouns**, which are names of people or places, are written with a capital letter. In German, all nouns are written with a capital letter.

NUMBER

In grammar, 'number' refers to how many there are of something. Often we need to show this grammatically by adding something to the word.

In English grammar there are only two numbers: singular (when there is only one of something) and plural (when there is more than one of something). Whenever we have more than one object, we normally show that by adding an '-s' to that word, as in the following example:

Singular (1)	Plural (2, 3, 4, 5+)
dog	dog<u>s</u>
cat	cat<u>s</u>

Although in English we only show number in the noun, in other languages you might need to show it in the adjective, the article and even the verb as well. Take a look at the following table:

English	French
the dog	le chien
the dogs	le<u>s</u> chien<u>s</u>
black dog	chien noir
black dogs	chiens **noir<u>s</u>**
A black dog? Where did you see him?	Un chien noir? Où tu l'as vu?

Black dogs? Where did you see them?	Des chiens noirs? Où tu **les** as **vus**?

Some languages can even have more than two numbers. For example, in addition to singular and plural, Hebrew also has the 'dual' form, which indicates that there are two of something:

	Singular (1)	**Dual (2)**	**Plural (3+)**
Hebrew	yom	yomáyim	yamim
English	day	two days	days

PREFIX/SUFFIX

Prefixes are added to the beginning and suffixes to the end of a word to change its meaning. They are especially important in languages like German, where an enormous quantity of words are formed by adding a prefix or suffix to a basic word.

English has them too, for example:

Prefix: dis-	Suffix: -able
discount	countable
disqualify	manageable
disobey	reachable
disgust	doable
disrespect	unthinkable

While in many cases the prefix or suffix have a clear purpose and effect on the meaning of a word, such as 'dis-' meaning to reverse or undo something, there are also examples of where that meaning has become blurred or forgotten by native speakers, such as the word 'disgust'. The word 'gust' is no longer used on its own in that context in the English language, but 'disgust' persists.

PREPOSITION

Prepositions are little words that appear before nouns or pronouns, which among other things are usually used to express a noun's location in time or space, or its relationship with other nouns.

<u>For example:</u>   in, on, at, to, for, of, from, by, with, about, between, along, etc.

Different languages rarely use the same prepositions as each other. Look out for differences in order to avoid making mistakes.

<u>For example:</u>   In English you would say that you are **on** the bus, but if you said that in German, that would mean that you are physically sitting on the roof. Instead, in German you should say that you are **in** the bus (*ich bin **im** Bus*). This makes sense in English, but it is not what a native speaker would naturally say.

Verbs often take prepositions in different languages, but again these can vary considerably.

<u>For example:</u>   In English you wait *for* someone, but in German you wait *on* someone (*ich warte **auf** dich*).

PRONOUN

Pronouns fill in for nouns when it's clear what you're talking about, or you don't want to repeat a word.

For example:	The <u>car</u> is blue.	[noun]
	<u>It</u> is blue.	[pronoun]
	Not only is that car blue, but <u>it</u> is even electric. [avoiding repetition]	

There are seven main types of pronoun:

1. **Personal pronouns**, which stand in for people.
   For example: I, you, she, he, it, we, they, us, them, me, her, him

2. **Relative pronouns**, which introduce **relative clauses**.
   For example: This is the car <u>that</u> I bought.

3. **Demonstrative pronouns**, which point out particular people or things.
   For example: this, that, these, those

4. **Indefinite pronouns**, for when we don't know who or what something is.
   For example: anyone, anything, something, someone

5. **Reflexive pronouns** are the ones that always end in '-self' or '-selves'.
   For example: Behave <u>yourself</u>!

6. **Interrogative pronouns** are question words for someone or something.
   For example: who, what, whose, which

7. **Possessive pronouns** show who something belongs to.
   For example: my, your, her, his, its, our, their, hers, mine, yours

SUBJECT/OBJECT

The 'subject' is the part of the sentence that does the verb. It is the opposite of the 'object' of a sentence, which is done by the verb.

For example:

subject	verb	object
The dog	caught	the ball.

In languages that have cases, in this example the subject 'the dog' would be in the nominative case, and the object 'the ball' would be in the accusative case. That is because in this example 'the ball' is a direct object.

Have a look at the indirect object in the example below:

subject	verb	object (indirect)	object (direct)
The dog	gives	the man	the bone.

An **indirect object** implies that you'll need a word like 'to', 'for' or 'at' in English. That is because the subject is indirectly performing the verb to the object, rather than directly being performed by it.

In our second example, the dog physically does something to the bone. He holds it in his teeth, and then drops it at the man's feet. The bone is physically altered, moved or affected by the verb, which makes it the **direct object**. The man, however, is not directly affected at all in this sentence. He is merely given the bone, and is therefore indirectly affected. That makes him the **indirect object**. If the language you're learning has the dative case, the indirect object will use it in this example.

In English there are also **prepositional objects**, or objects that require a preposition:

subject	verb	object (prepositional)
The dog	barks	at the skateboard.

The **prepositional object** is similar to the indirect object; it's just that it always requires a preposition. Often languages will have set rules about which prepositions verbs can take, and so it's a good idea to learn these at the same time that you learn the verb.

VERB

A verb is usually described as a 'doing word'. You can think of a verb as something that you do, or that can be done.

For example: choose, follow, decide, see, think, calculate

but not: ~~expectation, vision, tree, soft~~

Verbs can be divided into three categories: action, linking, and auxiliary.

Action verbs: to strike, to walk, to cook, to make, to decide, etc.

Linking verbs: The sky is blue. The dog seems happy. The sea appears calm.

Auxiliary verbs: I have seen it. She would do that. They had told me.

Some verbs can appear by themselves in a sentence, without needing to refer to an **object**. These are called **intransitive** verbs.

For example: I sit. I speak. I arrive. I sneeze. I work.

Other verbs that cannot appear without an **object** are called **transitive verbs**.

For example: I bring [*something*]. I catch [*the ball*]. I get [*good feedback*].

Some verbs can be *both* transitive and intransitive.

WORD ORDER

Languages structure information differently. As learners, this is something we have to look out for.

English has a fixed word order that hardly ever changes. This is called SVO (Subject–Verb–Object) word order.

1: Main Noun / Subject   2: Verb   3: Secondary Noun / Object

For example: **The dog** (S) **chews** (V) **the bone** (O).

Some languages also have fixed word orders, but use SOV (Subject–Object–Verb) instead.

For example: [Japanese] **Inu wa** (S) **hone o** (O) **kamimasu** (V).

        [lit.]   'Dog the bone the chews.'

Some languages, like Russian, Hungarian and Greek, have completely free word orders and often use **cases** to show where the subject and object of a sentence are. Any order is possible, but normally the most important information is put at the beginning or end of the sentence.

For example: [Hungarian] **A kutya** (S) **rágja** (V) **a csontot** (O).

        [lit.]   'The dog chews the bone.'

                  A csontot (O) **rágja** (V) **a kutya** (S).

        [lit.]   'The bone chews the dog.'

                  Rágja (V) **a kutya** (S) **a csontot** (O).

        [lit]   'Chews the dog the bone.'

In English, adjectives must always come before the noun. In other languages, the adjective may have to come after the noun.

For example: [English]   a white (adj.) car (n.)
                 [Hebrew]   oto (n.) levan (adj.)
                 [lit.]   'a car white'

The Three-Step Technique

It's harder to pinpoint specific methods for learning grammar as you can for vocabulary. The key really is to review things regularly and have constant contact with the language, so that the grammar gradually sinks in.

No matter how you approach it, you will find there are three key stages to learning grammar. Keep assessing where you are with each new topic. That way, you can stay aware of how much more work needs to be done.

Stage 1: Concept

The first thing you need to do is understand why a piece of grammar exists. Why does this particular instance require that construction? What is the need that this piece of grammar fulfils? Why is it that when you don't use it, it sounds like you're making a mistake?

This is called the **concept** of the grammar. Understanding the concept is your first challenge.

The best way to understand the concept is to read a description in your own language in a **grammar book**, or have a teacher explain it to you in your own language. Dwell on it, think it over, ask questions, and refer to examples and exceptions for greater clarification.

Stage 2: Memory

Your next task is to learn how to form a piece of grammar on your own. This will require you to memorise new endings or word orders that that particular piece of grammar demands.

TOP TIP: STUDY GRAMMAR IN YOUR OWN LANGUAGE

It is a widely held misconception that the best way to study a language is exclusively through the language you are learning. Grammar concepts can be most concisely and comprehensively conveyed through simple explanations in your own language. Studying grammar in a foreign language can double your workload: not only do you have to understand the grammar being taught, but also struggle to understand the actual language in which the explanation is presented to you.

Visual learners may find learning tables of information to be the most effective way of tackling this. **Auditory** or **kinaesthetic** learners could instead speak or write down the information on those tables in order for it to sink in.

One of the best ways to learn grammar is to memorise specific sentences or phrases that demonstrate the grammar in question. This is especially useful when you first encounter a grammar point in context, for example, from a reading or listening exercise on your course or in conversation.

Test yourself regularly with exercises that allow you to apply the grammar rule. Eventually you should aim to get the formation right each time.

Stage 3: Production

Finally, you now need to produce that grammar naturally, unprompted, and accurately. Once you have achieved that, you have mastered it. This is the last stage, and sometimes is the most elusive of all.

In the run-up, you should expect to make 'silly' mistakes and kick yourself because you knew it deep down. Sometimes you will get it right, other times you will slip up. Eventually you should aim to achieve 100 per cent accuracy. Remember though, each mistake you make is part of the learning process and is helping you to get there.

If you notice your accuracy decreasing and you start to make more mistakes, this is a sign that your language may be becoming rusty. Never shy away from 'topping up' your grammar by revising the concepts you learned in Stage 1, and re-doing exercises from Stage 2.

TOP TIP: REVIEW, REVIEW AND REVIEW AGAIN!

Language learning really never stops. Don't shy away from revisiting things you've already learned, even if you feel like you learned them well enough the first time. You can never be too thorough in your approach to grammar. It is always possible that there are exceptions or rules that escaped you the first time around. Think of it like taking your car to the mechanic every now and then to have things checked over and tightened up. Your language needs regular attention too!

Dealing with Irregularities

In most cases, grammar is simply a matter of learning a rule and knowing how and when to apply it. However, like everything, things don't always tend to run that smoothly.

Nearly all languages have exceptions, as well as rules. That means you can't just 'apply' a rule; you have to learn a new one instead.

When learning exceptions, bear two things in mind:

1. **The exceptions are always the minority of cases**. The vast majority of words that you learn will conform to the rules. Promise.

2. **The most irregular words are almost always the most common ones.** You will find yourself constantly coming across the exceptions, which will make it easier for you to remember them in the long term. That is in fact how they have remained irregular in the language.

DID YOU KNOW?

It is no coincidence that the most irregular words are the most common ones. If native speakers didn't keep hearing the exceptions, over time they would become regular.

In English, the past tense of 'help' and 'melt' used to be 'holp' and 'molt'. As these are not *very* common words, people gradually started saying 'helped' and 'melted', and so over time they became regular. However, the word 'molt' still survives in some specific phrases, such as 'molten lava'.

Using a Grammar Book

You will find a wealth of materials devoted solely to a language's grammar in any decent bookshop. These grammar books are usually thick, expensive, and don't always look that inviting. It may seem like the right place to start, but if your aim is to speak the language you're studying, you might want to hold off using one too much for now.

The majority of space in a grammar book is devoted to explaining exceptions, rather than rules. That means that if you try to work through a grammar book from cover to cover, you run the risk of getting lost in the detail of 5 per cent of cases, while losing sight of the 95 per cent.

Information is also usually laid out thematically so as to give the reader an overview of a topic, rather than introduced gradually and logically in keeping with a learner's needs at each stage.

Therefore, you'll nearly always be better off sticking to a course with a general approach that gives equal weight to vocabulary and grammar.

However, here are four instances in which getting out your grammar book is a good idea:

1. **When you have a question.** Most grammar books are designed to be used as a reference, rather than a course in their own right.

2. **When you keep making the same mistake.** That's a good sign that you have a knowledge gap, and checking the rule in your grammar book will be a good way to fill it up.

3. **If you want to learn about a language.** Not everyone wants to learn to speak, and for some people learning about the structure of a language is just as valuable.

4. **When you can't sleep.** Grammar books are great for insomnia.

TOP TIP: READ AHEAD

Finding out about a tricky piece of grammar before you get there in your course is a great way to start preparing for it. You can already start conceptualising it long before you know how to form it. You may also start being able to spot it in phrases that you have already learned.

Exercises

1. Open a random book in the language you are learning and start reading. Decide whether words are nouns, verbs, adjectives, adverbs, conjunctions or pronouns. What patterns do you notice emerging?

2. Take an average length sentence in your native language. Rewrite it as many times as you can, changing the word order. Which rules are you using each time?

3. Invent a new grammar rule in your native language. Read a short text and rewrite it showing this new grammar rule each time. Imagine how you would explain and teach this grammar rule to a student of your language.

Model Answers: Person E

1. *v.   adv.   adj.   n.   n.   n.   n. v.   n.*
Volt egyszer egy szegény favágó és annak felesége és két gyermeke: fiú volt az egyik,

   n.   n.   n.   v.   n.   adv.   adj.
lány a másik. A fiút Jancsikának hívták, a lánykát Juliskának. Nagyon szegény

   n.   v.   n.   conj. v.   n.   n.   conj.   conj.   v.
ember volt a favágó, mikor volt kenyér az asztalfiában, mikor nem és majd felvetette

   n.   adj. n.   v.   v.   n.   n.   n.   conj.
a gond szegény fejét: hogy tudja eltartani feleségét és két gyermekét. Este, mikor

   v.   pron.   v.   n.   adj. n.   n.   v.
lefeküdtek, mind ezen sóhajtozott a favágó és a nagy gondtól, bánattól be sem tudta

   v.   n.
hunyni a szemét.

Extract from 'Jánoska és Margitka', Hungarian folktale

2. At around two o'clock, I drink my second coffee of the day.
    At around two o'clock, I my second coffee of the day drink.
    At two o'clock around, I my second coffee of the day drink.
    At two o'clock around, I my second of the day coffee drink.
    At two o'clock around, I my coffee second of the day drink.
    At two o'clock around, I coffee my second of the day drink.
    Two o'clock at around, coffee my second of the day drink I.
    Two o'clock at around, my second of the day coffee drink I.
    Two o'clock at around, drink I my second coffee of the day.

3. Any verbs in 'reported' speech must appear in a different tense, to show they are not the opinion of the person speaking, by adding the '-alledge' suffix to the conjugated verb.

Original article: 'Bank to Leave London'
Workers awoke to the shock announcement that the Quartet group is to start moving to the continent. CEO Steven Baine told this newspaper banks simply 'could not wait' and 'would not risk' further uncertainty. The Quartet's new HQ will not be in Frankfurt or Dublin as had been expected, but Amsterdam. The Dutch city will offer the

US banking giant a high quality of life, give it easy access to the rest of Europe through Schiphol airport, and make available to it one of Europe's most multilingual and cosmopolitan workforces, according to the CEO.

Article with new grammar: 'Bank to Leavealledge London'
Workers awoke to the shock announcement that the Quartet group is to startalledge moving to the continent. CEO of the Quartet group Steven Baine told this newspaper banks simply 'couldalledge not wait' and 'wouldalledge not risk' further uncertainty. The Quartet's new HQ will not be in Frankfurt or Dublin as had been expected, but Amsterdam. The Dutch city will offeralledge the US banking giant a high quality of life, givealledge it easy access to the rest of Europe through Schiphol airport, and makealledge available to it one of Europe's most multilingual and cosmopolitan workforces, according to the CEO.

CHAPTER 6

Speaking

Of all the different skills that you develop when learning a new language, speaking can cause by far the most stress. Unlike reading or writing, when you speak you get very little time to order your thoughts, find the words, and produce the language. Many of us feel nervous about making mistakes and showing ourselves up, and everybody knows that feeling of anxiety when a word is on the tip of your tongue but won't quite come out.

When it goes well, though, speaking a foreign language can be a real pleasure. It sounds impressive to those around you, and being complimented by a native speaker on your language skills is the greatest boost that your motivation can have.

The Key to Speaking Any Language You Want

To speak any language you want, there is a barrier you must come through first. It's neither physical, nor is really to do with how much you have learned. It is an entirely psychological barrier that prevents you from speaking. The key to breaking it is: confidence.

In language learning terms, confidence is about feeling certain that you can do whatever you want. You can say what you need to say, and get what you need out of an interaction with another person.

The best way to start feeling confident is to keep proving to yourself that this is the case. Keep having conversations with other people in which you understand them and they understand you, and keep reminding yourself that although things may still be far from perfect, you are well on the way to speaking your new language fluently.

One approach to this is to immerse yourself in the foreign language. That means pack your bags, get on a plane and jump into the deep end by spending some time entirely surrounded by the language you're learning. This method is quite extreme, and you will certainly find it difficult to start off with. Eventually, though, you will find that you have no choice but to use the little bits of language that you do know, and then you will realise that you can do far more with it than you ever imagined. You will start having successful interactions, and these will motivate you to learn more and do more with your new language.

However, immersion is not always essential to developing confidence, and for many people it is not always practical. As long as you have regular interactions with the language and have the opportunity to speak, you will become confident regardless of where you are physically. This can be achieved through regular one-to-one lessons with a teacher (see Chapter 3).

Becoming confident is, ultimately, about acquiring the right mindset. Here are some questions to ask yourself that will set you on the right track:

★ WHAT'S THE WORST THING THAT CAN HAPPEN?

Your primary aim at all times is just to communicate. If you're making yourself understood and getting your point across, you're meeting it.

★ LOOK AT THE FUNNY SIDE OF LIFE

You're an adult. You know you're intelligent and can function in your own language. If in a foreign language you feel like your skills have been reduced now to those of a five-year-old, laugh. It's funny!

★ SMILE! (YOU'RE PROBABLY NOT ON CAMERA, THOUGH)

Body language is so important for communication. If you feel nervous before speaking, look the other person straight in the eye and smile. This will relax you, and make everything go more smoothly.

Making Mistakes

At school we are taught that mistakes are bad. They get marked in bright red pen, cause us to lose points in tests, and are used as a way of measuring our progress. This is a very damaging attitude, and unfortunately many of us take it with us into adult life.

When learning a language, mistakes can in fact turn out to be your best friends. The more embarrassing it is, the more likely you are to never make it again!

So rather than trying to avoid making mistakes, you should almost aim to make as many as possible. Like this, you create memorable situations that will lead to you remembering the right rule.

Of course, your objective is not to learn to speak with

mistakes imbedded in your language. Instead, the idea is to learn from those mistakes so that your language skills continue improving. But to do this, first it's important to understand the kind of mistakes that you're making to then work out how to fix them.

Mistakes fall into one of two categories:

1. SLIPS

These happen when you *do* know what you should have said, but your mouth worked faster than your brain and the wrong thing came out.

2. KNOWLEDGE GAPS

These happen because you simply don't know the right word or piece of grammar that you need, and so are unavoidable.

If you find yourself making lots of 'slips' when you speak, then don't worry too much. The problem is not your knowledge of the language, but your ability to produce it spontaneously and accurately under pressure. This is something that comes with a lot of practice and exposure. As long as you're creating regular opportunities to use the language, you are on the right track to fixing it.

If you're suffering from 'knowledge gaps', that's a sign that you need to revise some things more carefully. But don't be hard on yourself – there's no way you could have got it right, as you simply have never learned the rule! Your teacher should be able to identify your knowledge gaps and suggest ways for you to fill them.

HOW TO SPEAK ANY LANGUAGE FLUENTLY

DID YOU KNOW?

Many of us make mistakes even while speaking our own language. These largely go undetected, though, because we speak our own language so confidently that the other person might just think they've misheard. Remember, not all mistakes will lead to you being misunderstood, so instead focus on your delivery and start speaking!

Accents

Accent is the way in which you speak a language. It does not refer to how you produce individual sounds (see Pronunciation), but instead to the overall shade of colour that you give the language when you speak it. Accents can be categorised by all sorts of criteria, such as region, class and age. However, as individuals, everybody has their own individual accent – both in their native language, and in the languages that they learn.

It is extremely rare for adults to learn to speak a non-native language without any trace of foreign accent. Normally for this to happen, they would have to be stationed where the foreign language is spoken for a very long time or from a young age. Ironically, those who do sound native in another language may even end up acquiring a foreign accent in their mother tongue.

This is because accent is largely based on the shape of the muscles in your mouth, and from where you are used to forming sounds. As your mouth is normally 'set up' to pronounce your native language, completely transforming this shape in order to accommodate a new language is a strain that is hard to maintain in the long run.

Yet, despite how good it might sound to the untrained ear, having a convincing accent in a foreign language can still leave many other things exposed. In fact, there are even several reasons why having a foreign accent could actually be to your advantage:

★ **SOUNDING FOREIGN SHOWS YOU ARE NOT LOCAL**
People will therefore not expect you to be fully aware of cultural norms and be more forgiving about faux-pas and mistakes (see Chapter 10).

★ **FOREIGN ACCENTS CAN SOUND EXOTIC AND EVEN ATTRACTIVE**
On the other hand, bear in mind that grammar mistakes do not always sound attractive (see Chapter 5).

★ **IT SHOWS THAT YOU'VE WORKED ON THE LANGUAGE**
You weren't born speaking it and have had to put in a considerable effort to get as far as you have. This nearly always impresses people, and they will compliment you for it.

WHICH ACCENT TO CHOOSE?

Another problem with having a 'native-sounding' accent is that you may not always be aware of the cultural implications of the one you have chosen. You may inadvertently be adopting an identity that you do not have in your native language. Many learners of English model their accent on the aristocratic tones of the British royal family, yet on visiting the UK are shocked to discover that this is not always received well by local people, who might (wrongfully) assume they share the political beliefs and attitudes of the country's most privileged upper classes.

HOW TO SPEAK ANY LANGUAGE FLUENTLY

If you do want to work towards obtaining a native-like accent, always model your pronunciation on somebody that you know and like in order to avoid this.

Pronunciation

Pronunciation refers directly to the way in which you produce individual sounds. It is not necessary to completely reproduce sounds as accurately as a native speaker, but if sounds are mispronounced then that could lead to you not being understood properly.

Learning to pronounce a new language is about *approximating* new sounds as best you can. As long as you are *consistent* and *clear* in the way that you speak, people will have no problems understanding you.

To improve your pronunciation:

★ **RECORD YOURSELF**

Then compare your version with a native speaker's. Repeat this, each time trying to sound closer to the original.

★ **MINIMAL PAIRS**

These are two words that sound similar but have a subtle difference. Hearing and then pronouncing these words one after the other can help you to hear the difference. For example, confusing 'u' and 'ü' in German is a common mistake that could lead to complicated misunderstandings:

schwül – humid, sticky   *schwul* – homosexual

★ SINGING

We tend to exaggerate our pronunciation while singing, and so this can be a good way to train up your mouth muscles. Also sounds in song can be less muffled and more easily distinguished than in speech.

★ UNDERSTAND HOW TO FORM THE SOUNDS

There are often useful descriptions and sometimes diagrams at the start of most self-taught language courses. Also ask your teacher to demonstrate the differences between sounds for you.

WHAT IS THE INTERNATIONAL PHONETIC ALPHABET?

The IPA has been used by linguists since 1888 to try to represent every sound in every language on Earth. This can be a great way to learn to pronounce words in languages with more complicated systems of spelling, like French, Russian and Thai. You can also use it to work out which sounds you already know from your first language, and which ones are new.

As the IPA is largely based on the Latin alphabet that we use in English, it's not too difficult to learn. There are plenty of free resources readily available on YouTube and the rest of the internet that will help you get to grips with it.

Intonation

This is by far the most important aspect of pronunciation, and one of the easiest to learn. Rather than individual sounds, intonation is the **melody** of the language. It refers to when words in a sentence are higher or lower pitched than others.

We use different pitches to convey the tone of what we are saying, such as emphasis, emotions, attitude, to be ironic or express surprise, pose questions, and express politeness. In tonal languages like Chinese and Swedish, it is even used to distinguish the meaning of different words.

Every language has set rules and conventions about when to lower or raise the pitch of your speech. If you learn these and use them correctly, you will greatly increase your chances of being understood by native speakers, regardless of how strong your accent is or even if you make mistakes.

As when learning pronunciation, listen carefully to the tone people use in the language you're learning use to express surprise, ask questions, make statements, greet each other and so on. These are usually wildly different, even between languages that are similar.

For example, most European languages use a raised intonation to form a question, such as in Spanish:

Statement: Tú quieres agua.   Question: ¿Tú quieres agua?

Some languages can be remarkably flat in their intonation, like Hungarian:

Statement: Nem akar vizet inni. Question: Nem akar vizet inni?

Others can be extremely rich in tone, and feel almost unnaturally song-like, such as Hebrew:

S: Hu lo rotze lishtot mayim.   Q: Hu lo rotze lishtot mayim?

Don't worry, these patterns are much more intuitive when they're heard than written down!

Body Language and Non-Verbal Communication

Over half of the way we communicate is through body language. And yet, there's a temptation when speaking a foreign language to concentrate so much on getting the words right that you can forget about everything else.

Your first few conversations in a new language are always likely to be stressful, as it takes time to get used to speaking. Your posture and body language might show this if you're not careful, which could lead to further misunderstandings.

If you feel nervous before starting a conversation in your new language, try taking a deep breath, relax, and concentrate on these things:

1. EYE CONTACT

Remember to maintain natural eye contact with the person you're speaking to. Even if you're struggling to remember words, looking at the person rather than the floor will give you a better chance of making yourself understood.

2. SMILE!

Not only will this make you more relaxed, but an apologetic smile can win over the other person and make them more patient and understanding. Remember, people always appreciate you making the effort to learn their language.

3. GESTURES

At the beginning stages there really are no rules about what you're allowed to do to make yourself understood. Point and mime as much as you like to reinforce what you're saying! In fact if you don't know a word, this is a great way to find out what it is in the moment.

4. REPEAT OR SLOW DOWN

Don't be afraid to ask someone to say something again or slower. This is not an exam, and you don't lose anything by being doubly sure you understand!

TOP TIP: WATCH THEIR BODY LANGUAGE, TOO

Remember too that body language goes both ways. When having a conversation in a foreign language you should be watching the other person at least as much as you're listening to them. You will surprise yourself with how much you can guess of what people mean without understanding what they are saying!

Learn It Like You Want to Speak It

One of the largest gaps to bridge when learning a new language is between what you are taught, and what you need to say. It is entirely possible to develop a very good theoretical or passive understanding of a language, but be unable to speak it spontaneously when the moment comes.

One way this can happen is if you focus on studying topics that don't directly relate to you. For example, if you don't plan to cook or go food shopping in the country where they speak your language, memorising endless lists of words like onions, red onions, peppers, plums and pineapples is not going to be that useful.

However, one of the few times when a word might come in handy is if you need to say: 'I don't like pineapples.' In that case, try learning exactly that phrase. That way, you are preparing yourself for a real-life conversational situation, and saving yourself the trouble of having to come up with that construction on the spot. This will make everything flow a lot better.

With every word that you learn, imagine a situation in which you would realistically use it. Think about where you'd be, whom you'd be talking to, and what you'd be saying about it. Then learn that word as part of a phrase you can imagine yourself using.

PREPARE FOR CONVERSATIONS

Write down a list of conversation topics that you would like to be able to talk about. For example: work, family, education, hobbies, travels, food, politics, etc. For each one, make as detailed a mind-map as possible of all the different things you'd like to say about the topic. Then identify which words you already know, and which ones you'll have to learn to be able to say what you want.

Receiving Feedback and Corrections

When you're in the middle of speaking, you might not be in the best frame of mind to be corrected on a mistake you've made. You're focused on the task at hand. As long as you've been understood, getting muddled about a tense or a gender shouldn't be too much of a concern. However, whether you welcome it or not, some people you speak to will automatically correct you.

Firstly, remember that in most cases this is not necessarily meant to be a criticism. There are all sorts of scenarios in which things get misunderstood (including between native speakers), and it's very normal for someone to repeat back what they've understood without even realising how this might come across as patronising.

With that in mind, try not to let it put you off. Now is not the time to be worrying about perfection. As a minimum, make a mental note of what has been corrected, and in your next study session try to look up the mistake you made in a grammar book or ask your teacher if you want to understand why you made that mistake.

If you're confident that you do know that rule and are certain that you just got things mixed up, then it's simply a case of needing more practice before you start getting it right first time, all the time. The good news is that the experience of getting it wrong and being corrected has just brought you a few steps closer to getting it right next time.

If someone does correct you mid-sentence, assume that they're trying to help. Smile, and thank them. Then, to make sure you remember the correction, repeat what they've said back to them to check that you heard them correctly. It can also be helpful to learn a phrase to use in this situation, such as 'So is that how I'm supposed to say it?'

'Shall We Just Speak in English?'

English is the modern world's de facto lingua franca. Nowadays, no matter where you go, you are more likely to find someone who speaks English than any other language. And many times, when you are trying your hardest to speak someone else's language, you will no doubt have been asked 'Shall we just speak in English?'

It can be extremely disheartening, but try to think about why it is happening. At first you might think it's because you're speaking the language badly, but in fact there are a number of things at play. Remember also that this is not something that just happens to native English speakers – language learners of all nationalities are faced with this same problem.

★ YOU'RE A TOURIST
And that means that you're probably in tourist areas. In many countries it is compulsory to speak English in order to work in the tourism sector. People working there may just be in the habit of speaking English and not notice you're speaking their language.

★ PEOPLE WANT TO PRACTISE ENGLISH
Just as you might learn a language that's not commonly spoken where you live, when local people have the opportunity to practise some English, they jump at it.

★ SPEAKING ENGLISH IS A POINT OF PRIDE
Many people pride themselves on having worked hard to learn English. They see it as a sign of their hospitality or education.

To rescue this situation, here are some different strategies you can employ:

1. KEEP SPEAKING THEIR LANGUAGE BACK
Although you might end up in the bizarre situation where you're both determinedly speaking each other's language and nobody gives any ground.

2. SAY SOMETHING TO THEM

Learn a nice phrase like 'Thank you so much for speaking English, but I've come to your country to learn your language and so I'd really appreciate it if you'd let me practise it.' This should work in most cases.

3. JUST PRETEND NOT TO UNDERSTAND THEM

This is not for the faint-hearted, and can often feel mean. But if you're in touch with that slightly evil streak in you then it can actually work quite well. Turn the situation round on them and suddenly they'll feel like their English is the problem. As you'll see, they'll switch back to speaking their language in no time!

Language Etiquette

There are some unwritten rules when it comes to speaking different languages. By following these, both in your own country and abroad, you will help people all around the world to enjoy learning languages more.

The main idea is that if somebody approaches you and tries to speak your language in your country, you can assume that they have travelled quite a long way and invested a considerable amount of money to practise your language with you.

No matter how incomprehensible they sound, or how much they struggle to understand you, always allow the conversation to be carried out in the language of the place that you are in. Be patient, use hand gestures, and allow the other person to get there in their own time. The other person won't remember the excruciating difficulty of the conversation that you will, but instead will focus on the fact that they successfully managed to ask for information, get it, and understand in the language that they are learning. If this scenario unfolds in front of family and friends, all the better. Give them the chance to be proud of their beloved 'linguist' family member.

Never press the 'should we just speak your language?' button except as an absolute last resort. It won't be received well, and the other person will rightfully be quite offended in thinking that you didn't think they spoke your language very well.

Doing this creates good karma for language learners everywhere. You never know, one day that may come in handy for you!

Finding People to Speak With

If you are living in a foreign country, the chances are that you're surrounded by people to practise speaking with, and who will want to learn your language as well. If you're in your own country, though, this can be a little harder.

To put everything from this chapter into practice, you will need to find opportunities to speak. Here are some places to start looking:

1. MEET-UPS

These are quite informal events where people come to practise a language. They are usually specific to one language, but can also be more broadly for people interested in different languages. The best place to look is meetup.com, but also look up 'speaking clubs' or 'meetup groups' on Google for your language and you're bound to find others too.

2. LANGUAGE EXCHANGES

If you want to learn the language of someone who wants to learn yours, you're in a great position to set up a Language Exchange. Normally you might meet for an hour and devote 30 minutes to speaking each language.

To get the most out of this, it's always a good idea to:

★ Both be at a similar level in each other's language, so you can have conversations about the same sorts of things.

★ Plan and agree in advance what you're going to talk about.

★ Discuss things like corrections, accent, and what you'd like to concentrate on beforehand.

3. ONLINE

If you don't know anybody to meet up with where you live, the internet is full of people who can help you learn their language. Online exchanges work exactly the same as offline ones, the only difference is that you meet on Skype rather than in a café. The fact that you're both potentially in totally different parts of the world can in itself lead to some fascinating and memorable conversations! Italki.com is a great place to find online language partners. There are also many language-learning groups on Facebook that are full of people who want to help.

Getting Around Knowledge Gaps

The hardest challenge when speaking is either not knowing or not remembering the right words. This can lead to a lot of frustration, which might even throw you off in the heat of the moment.

Not remembering words is a part of life, and something that many of us do even in our own language. When speaking a foreign language, it's important to accept that it happens more regularly, and can seem like more of a problem than in our first language.

When you simply don't know a word, a lot of frustration can come from not being able to express yourself exactly as you'd like. As adults, we're used to the luxury of having a fully formed native language that we can mould to fit our needs. As language learners, we need to learn to make compromises.

As you progress with your new language, you will feel more confident using it, but also notice every now and then that there are words you simply do not know. For example, let's say you're in France and you drop your wallet into the gutter. You know the word for 'wallet': *'portefeuille'*, but you don't know the word for 'dropped'. However, you do know the word for 'fell': *'est tombé'*. This means 90 per cent the same thing as dropped, and gets your point across.

The one you don't know is 'gutter'. Here it's an extremely important word, because it tells us how urgent it is to rescue it before it gets ruined. So how can you get around this knowledge gap?

1. You could just say 'street': *'rue'*, but that probably only covers at best 20 per cent of the meaning and does not imply that it is currently swimming in mud and rain water.

2. You could say 'the side of the street': *'le côté de la rue'*, but again this is far too clean for what's actually happened, and only captures around 40 per cent of the meaning.

HOW TO SPEAK ANY LANGUAGE FLUENTLY

3. Finally, you can describe where your wallet fell in as much detail using words you know to explain 'gutter': *'Mon portefeuille est tombé dans la partie de la rue avec tous les excréments!'* 'The part of the road with all the excrement' is 90 per cent the meaning of 'gutter', and completely gets your point across.

Option 3 is called 'Talking Around Your Vocab Gaps'. Be as creative as you can, and use all of the vocabulary that you remember to get your point across. At times this can be exaggerated or alarming, but as long as you're understood, you're not breaking any rules. The best thing about this is that after listening to your vivid description, someone will probably say *'Ah, vous voulez dire dans un* **caniveau***?'* – 'Ah, you mean in the gutter?', at which point you have a wonderfully vivid opportunity to learn a new word.

Exercises

1. Ask your teacher or language partner to keep a note of all of the mistakes you've made in a lesson, and give this to you at the end. Decide which mistakes are simply slips, and which are knowledge gaps.

2. Listen to a recording on YouTube of someone reciting a poem. Find the text, and record yourself saying it. Note down all of the difference between your pronunciation and theirs, then re-record yourself trying to get closer to the original.

3. Spend the next week focusing as much as possible on your body language and non-verbal communication. Breathe out before you start speaking, and hold yourself upright and with confidence while you talk. Note how easier it becomes to speak the language, and any other differences you notice.

4. Find a way to fit an extra thirty minutes of conversation practice per week into your routine. Look for meetup events near you, or find a conversation partner online.

5. Choose ten complicated words that you do not know in the language you are learning. Come up with strategies for 'talking around' these knowledge gaps.

Model Answers: Person F

1.

Mistake	Correction	Explanation	Type
~~le avion~~	l'avion	*le* and *la* become *l'* in front of a vowel sound	*slip*
~~j'ai allé~~	je suis allé	some verbs take *être* to form the past tense instead of *avoir*	*gap*
~~j'ai arrivé~~	je suis arrivé	some verbs take *être* to form the past tense instead of *avoir*	*gap*
~~vous faisez~~	vous faites	*faire* is an irregular verb	*slip*
~~actuellement~~	en fait	*actuellement* is a false friend: in French it means 'currently' not 'actually'	*gap*
~~je suis faim~~	j'ai faim	in French you 'have' hunger	*slip*
~~cettes filles~~	ces filles	the fem. word for 'this' is *cette*, but the fem. word for 'these' is not *cettes*, but *ces*	*gap*
~~j'ai venu~~	je suis venu	some verbs take *être* to form the past tense instead of *avoir*	*gap*

2. Person F notices that after 'ee', there can be an 'h' sound. The word 'yes' ('oui') is not pronounced 'wee', but 'weehh'. He notices that the word 'beaucoup' is made of two different sounds. It's not [boo-koo], but more like [bow-koo]. Person F could never do the French 'r', but when he thinks more about pronunciation, he starts making sounds from the back of his mouth and everything becomes easier. Pronunciation is just about having your mouth form the right shape.

3. Person F takes a deep breath through his nose, breathes out slowly through his mouth, and smiles. He repeats this until he feels relaxed, and then starts speaking. He does this again if he feels stressed. This makes him feel in control, and he makes fewer mistakes. People respond to him more patiently and more positively than before too.

4. Person F found a group of lower-intermediate French learners on the internet, who were planning on meeting not too far from him. He thought everyone would be better than him, but they were all friendly and open to practising French.

5.

Complicated word	Way to 'talk around' it
steering wheel	'where you sit when you are driving the car'
dustpan and brush	'small thing to clean rubbish from the floor with'
bucket	'plastic thing for water'
skirting board	'long part at the bottom of the wall'
radiator	'hot thing' or 'warm thing'
sieve	'something to put this in to lose the water'
charger	'something to put battery in my phone'
submarine	'boat that swims under the water'
awning	'thing over the top to protect from the sun'
grater	'thing to make little pieces of cheese'

CHAPTER 7

Listening

Listening is one of the hardest skills to develop when learning a new language. No matter how many different techniques you try out, it just takes time before you start seeing results.

Training Your Ear

The good news is that despite needing the most time, nowadays listening is probably the skill you can practise the most. You will automatically be improving your listening every time you interact with another person in that language, both in casual conversation and also in lessons. If you have a smartphone or MP3 player, you can practise listening wherever and whenever you like. Listening is the one activity that can fill all of the 'dead time' you identified in your routine in Chapter 1.

One of the reasons why improving your listening is so slow is that as adults we learn languages back to front. Instead of learning to understand, speak, then read and write, we focus on the written word far earlier than when we learn languages as children. That means that we tend to recognise words when they're written down far more easily than when we hear them.

There are many reasons why it makes sense to learn in that way, such as having access to dictionaries and other resources much earlier, but it does mean that a gap can open up between what you can read and what you can hear. Some languages like Spanish are very easy to read if you speak another Romance language or English. But if you try to listen in to what a Spanish speaker is saying, then suddenly you have a very different challenge at hand.

This is why it is so important to be patient, and remember that this takes time. There are ways in which to bridge this gap, but the key is to take it slow and steady.

Knowing What to Listen Out For

Listening in a foreign language is a very different task to listening in your native language. But before we start discussing the skills and techniques you'll need to develop, the first challenge to overcome is your mindset.

In your new language, you will have to accept that you won't reach the degree of 100 per cent understanding that you have in your native language. There will always be words that you miss or don't know, and you will have to ask people to repeat themselves.

But even if 100 per cent understanding is off the cards, as long as you know *what* to listen out for, with time you can still get very close to that.

When you start listening in a new language, try to listen out for the following three things, in this order:

1. GIST

You won't be able to provide a word-for-word translation of what someone's saying, but how much can you guess from what you do understand? How much is obvious from the situation, their body language, and tone of voice?

2. DETAIL

Once you understand the basics, you can start honing in on the specifics. Start listening out for **when**, **who**, **how many**, **where**, and as much as you can to create a more complete picture of what's being said.

3. WORDS

Once you've mastered Steps 2 and 3, what's left are the words that you don't understand. Only by this stage will you start being able to hear them clearly and remember them. Make a note of the words you can make out, along with the gist and detail of the conversation where you heard them, and use your next study period to look them up.

WHAT IS DICTATION?

Dictation is one of the oldest language learning methods around. Your teacher will read out a passage in the language you are learning, and you will write it down as you hear it. It doesn't matter whether you actually understand what's being said, as this isn't a comprehension exercise. Here you are focusing on your listening and writing skills. It's a good idea to hear the passage several times: once without stopping, and then once with the teacher pausing at the end of each sentence. You can swap out your teacher by using a podcast or other audio recording for a dictation instead. Just pause at opportune moments, and make sure you have somebody who can check what you've written.

Dictations

This is a very traditional way of developing listening skills, and nowadays might seem a little old-fashioned. However, although it certainly isn't the only way to develop listening skills, there are still a lot of ways it can help.

Dictation really helps you to connect the written to the spoken word. If you're doing a lot of study from books and don't hear natural speech that often, this might be exactly what you need to realise that you've been mispronouncing words in your head as you read them, and to help you distinguish between different sounds that you're not used to, like Hungarian's vowel trilogies of o, ó, ő and u, ú, ű.

Alternatively, it might make you realise that sounds you thought were pronounced differently are actually pronounced the same. In French, for example, spelling hardly ever matches up with sound, but there are many different ways to spell the same sound. 'eau', 'au', 'ault', 'o', 'ô', 'ot', 'os', and 'op' are all pronounced like the 'o' in 'cold'.

You may also find out that even in so-called 'phonetic' languages, where words are generally spelled like they sound, there are plenty of exceptions. In Russian, the word for 'five' is spelled 'пять' (pyat), but actually pronounced more like 'петь' (pyet). The word 'петь' (pyet) already exists in Russian and means 'to sing', but is often pronounced more like 'пить' (pyit). 'Пить' (pyit) is the Russian word 'to drink'. On paper, you would never get these confused. In speech though, they are something you really should listen out for.

Finally, apart from listening, dictations are a great way to practise writing and spelling in the language that you're learning. This, as we've seen from our examples, might not always be that straightforward. They're also a great alternative to simply reading through a text with your teacher, as they really make you concentrate on each word which in turn makes them more memorable when you come to sitting down and learning vocabulary from them.

Suggest to your teacher that you incorporate these into your lessons and spend about thirty minutes on dictation every other week.

Podcasts

A podcast is by far one of the most useful and most widely available resources that there are for learning a new language. If you use a smartphone or portable MP3 player like an iPod, you are free to take these with you everywhere and listen into them wherever and whenever you have a moment. This allows you to really make use of your 'dead time' unlike anything else.

When learning a language outside of the country where it is spoken, you will find yourself almost swimming against the tide to make use of the limited amount of time you can spend studying, and really make it count. If you have no exposure to the language outside of your study time, inevitably you will slowly start forgetting things you have learned until you come across them again. The moment you close your books is the moment you 'switch off' all of your exposure to that language.

When you are in an 'immersed' environment (where the language you are learning is spoken all around you), there are reminders for what you've been learning everywhere – on street signs, in conversations that you overhear, whenever you turn on the TV, and so on. With a phone or iPod loaded with foreign language podcasts, you can almost recreate what that feels like from anywhere in the world.

Aside from their portability, the real power of podcasts is that unlike live radio or TV, they only run for a specific length of time. They can be as short as ten minutes, as long as an hour or perhaps even more. But just knowing how long something will last before you commit to listening to it can really work to your advantage. You can choose one that will last as long as you'll be spending on the bus, doing household chores, or accompany you as you head out for a long walk or a run.

TOP TIP: SLOW NEWS

Keeping up with the pace of real audio recordings is one of the biggest challengers for language learners. Fortunately, there are resources out there that slow everything down, so you can take your time to work out what's being said. The *News In Slow* series offers podcasts in French, German, Italian and Spanish (www.NewsInSlow.com). For German learners, the news site Deutsche Welle also offers a slow news service amongst its many other resources for people interested in the German language (www.dw.de).

There is a huge choice of podcasts available designed both for native speakers and for learners. Nearly all major news channels around the world produce podcasts in addition to their broadcast services, such as the BBC in the UK, Deutsche Welle in Germany, RTVE in Spain and Ekho Moskvy in Russia. These are a great source of natural language aimed at real native speakers, but in order to get more than just the rhythm of the language and the occasional familiar word, you will probably need to be at a fairly advanced stage of your language learning to really engage with them.

Although not as 'authentic', podcasts that are created for non-native speakers can be of huge value to you in your studies. The language they use is simplified, with the aim of teaching particular vocabulary or grammar topics each time, and many come with additional learning materials available online, such as glossaries and transcriptions.

> ## IS THIS TOO HARD FOR MY LEVEL?
> Whether it's a new textbook, a new podcast, or even just a new teacher or conversation partner, whenever you switch to a new language 'input source' it's extremely common to feel that you are struggling. That doesn't mean that you have 'gone backwards' or 'forgotten' anything you've learned, it's just that you've been prepared by whatever you were using before to understand a certain type of language, which may be different in your new source. There will be a transition period, but as long as you persist you will easily manage to fill any gaps in vocabulary and before long be back up to where you feel you should be.

Radio

Much of what can be said about podcasts also applies to listening to the radio. With mobile apps like TuneIn, internet radio also allows you to take it with you on your phone as you would do a podcast. The only obvious main differences are that radio is an endless stream of broadcasting, while podcasts are finite, and with podcasts you have to choose what you want to listen to, while with the radio you just switch it on and listen to whatever's on.

Foreign-language radio is a great thing to have on in the background when you're at home. It will help you adjust your ear to the rhythm, melody and sound of the language, as well as occasionally giving you that much needed feeling of achievement when you recognise a word or phrase that you hear and understand what it means.

The radio can also help introduce you to music in the language that you're learning, which in turn can help you to learn vocabulary (see Chapter 4). If you hear a song that you like and want to listen to again but didn't catch what it's called, an app called 'Shazam' available for most smartphones will help you to identify it by listening in to a short extract and telling you its name and who the artist is.

As with podcasts, the real strength of foreign language radio and its global availability through the internet is that it allows you to tune in and out whenever is convenient, and increase your overall exposure to the language that you're learning. In doing so, you're also more likely to hear words being repeated, which in turn will make them more memorable.

DON'T JUST LISTEN, LISTEN ACTIVELY

Rather than allowing the language to just wash over you, you can make listening to podcasts or the radio an active learning activity too. Sit and listen for twenty to thirty minutes with a pad of paper and a pen in front of you. Write down new vocabulary and phrases that you hear and look them up later. Listen out for words and phrases that you don't know, and also ones you do know but wouldn't have used in that context. Make notes on anything you hear that's interesting, and actively listen out for things to write down. Later on, try to summarise what you've heard by explaining it to your language exchange partner or teacher.

Watching TV/Films

For visual learners, TV and film has the edge. It has many of the benefits of radio and podcasts, but with the one crucial difference that it offers visual aids as well. Based on what you can see, it becomes easier to guess from the context what new words mean, and in the longer term will make them far more memorable.

As so much TV from around the world is now available online, you no longer have to be in the country in order to watch films and shows in a different language. Many series are available on YouTube, and most major broadcasters have services online, like the BBC's iPlayer, ZDF's Mediathek in Germany, and RTVE en directo in Spain. Some of these require you to be physically in the country in order to access all of their services, but this can often be overcome if you use a VPN client on your computer that will trick the website into thinking that you are actually in the country.

You may think that you'd be best starting off by watching something like the news, but realistically you will not be able to understand much of what is being said. Instead, you should try first watching children's TV, especially shows that actually teach things like the alphabet or animals to kids. Be wary of watching cartoons, though, as these may be poorly dubbed from English.

PLAY THE ADVERT GAME

Adverts are designed to be fun, engaging, and most importantly for language learners, memorable. That means that they can be an excellent way to learn new vocabulary by watching TV. You will see these if you're able to watch live TV where you are, otherwise plenty of adverts are uploaded to YouTube or other video streaming sites.

You can turn this into a fun, language-related game, in which you even learn a lot about a country's culture and values. Try to predict what is being advertised before the end of the clip, making a note of key words or slogans that are used, and see if you are right!

Subtitles and Dubbing

If you've ever watched a foreign film in your own country, it will either have been subtitled or dubbed into your own language, so that it could be understood by a local audience.

Reading subtitles can allow you to hear the original but have a simultaneous live translation of what's going on. However, in order to make sure you do also listen to the audio, keep a pad of paper next to you to take notes and as you're watching ask yourself:

★ Have you found any words/phrases that you didn't know?
★ Do any words or expressions keep coming up? If so, when?
★ Have you spotted any differences between what you can understand from the audio and what you've read in the subtitles?

Always take the time afterwards to go through your notes and look up any words you're not sure about. Remember too that subtitles are not always precise, as sometimes words or expressions do not have a one-for-one translation in other languages. Subtitles also need to be more concise for practical reasons, which means many fillers such as 'and so ...' 'well ...' 'what I mean is ...', which you use to make your language sound more authentic, get dropped.

When a film is dubbed that means that the original audio track is replaced with the voices of different actors reading the script in a different language. This is usually lip-synced as much as possible to the original, but obviously cannot always fully match up. In some countries, such as Spain, Germany and Poland, there is not much of a tradition of reading subtitles, and so almost all films and TV series from abroad are dubbed, while in others such as the Netherlands and Greece you can be hard-pressed to find anything on TV that isn't subtitled!

Generally speaking, dubbing is not particularly useful for learning a new language. However, if you take a film that you know very well in your own language, watching it dubbed into the language you're learning can be useful. When you already know what happens and what people are supposed to be saying when, you're free to just concentrate on the workings of the language instead.

HOW TO USE AND GRADUALLY LOSE SUBTITLES

Using subtitles to watch a film in a foreign language is like wearing arm-bands when you first start learning to swim: they get you in the pool, but your aim should be to learn to live without them as quickly as you can.

1. Put subtitles in your native language on whichever film you watch. This will enable you to have 100% comprehension. Try to focus on what you hear being said, and try to match it with what you're reading in the subtitles. Make a note of any new vocabulary that you pick up.

2. Once you understand 50% or more of the audio, switch the subtitles over to the language that you're learning. That means that you are simultaneously reading *and* hearing what the language. Make notes to help you follow what's going on, and feel free to pause and look words up if you feel really lost. This stage is hard, but really useful for your language learning.

3. Once you understand 75% or more by using subtitles in the language, it's time to switch them off completely. This is quite a leap, and it's a good idea to keep very detailed notes of new words you hear so you can look them up later. This will be easier for you if you've been practising dictation (see p. 107). You may find that you need to turn subtitles back on for subjects that you are less fluent in. Feel free to dip in and out of stages 2 and 3 until you are completely subtitle-free.

Exercises

1. Listen to a dialogue, a short interview, podcast or radio show and make notes on what is being said. Afterwards, prepare a short, thirty-second summary in the language you are learning of everything that you heard.

2. Listen to a recording of natural speech, such as an interview. Write down any phrases you hear being used repeatedly. Before you look these up, try to guess what they might mean based on the tone of the speaker's voice and any other context.

3. While listening to a recording, think of five to ten questions you would like to ask the speaker based on what they are saying.

4. Watch an episode of a TV programme in your target language that you like with subtitles, and make an estimate of how much you understood as a percentage. Then re-watch the episode but without subtitles, and see how much more or less you understood.

5. Aim to listen to natural speech in the language you're learning through internet radio or podcasts for at least thirty minutes per week. Try to pick out words and phrases you understand, and write down ones you can hear that you don't understand.

Model Answers: Person G

1. Person G is learning Dutch with a podcast in which everyday people tell real stories from their lives. Here are her notes:

Dutch notes	English translation
Met beste vriendin, praten over liefde	With best friend, talking about love
Zij was nooit verliefd	She's never been in love
Als zij zoent met een knappe jongen op vakantie en ervan een foto maakt, krijgt ze een euro	If she kisses a good-looking boy on holiday and takes a photo of it, she'll get a euro
Ontmoet een jongen op vakantie	Meets a nice boy on holiday
Jongen vraagt: wil je me zoenen?	Boy asks: Do you want to kiss me?
Zij zoenen, een fijne, gevoelige zoen	They kiss: a nice, passionate kiss
Ze weet ze gaat hem missen	She knows she's going to miss him
Volgende dag zit ze in de auto leeg en verdrietig, toen wist ze, zo voelt verliefd	Next day in the car empty and sad. Realises how it feels to be in love

2.

Dutch	English
liefde	love
een knappe jongen	a handsome boy
de zoen	the kiss
de weddenschap	the bet
verliefd	in love

3.

Dutch	English
Wat zei je vriendin, toen jullie terug komen?	What did your friend say when you got back?
Waarom is het zo belangrijk voor tieners om hun eerste zoen te hebben?	Why is it so important for teenagers to have their first kiss?
Wat zou je ouders adviseren die kinderen hebben die verliefd zijn?	What advice do you give to parents who have children who are in love?

4. Person G is watching a Dutch reality TV show called *Wie is de Mol?*. The language is mainly basic conversation between the candidates expressing their feelings. With subtitles, Person G understands more than 75% of the programme. When she turns subtitles off, things get harder. She's distracted by the different sounds and can't tell when one word starts and ends. However, as she has watched it before, she can work out most things and realises she knows more words than she thought.

5. Person G feels gratified at recognising so many of the phrases she hears, but also writes down a lot of new ones that she wants to learn. She looks these up on the internet to find English equivalents.

CHAPTER 8

Reading

Reading in a foreign language is one of the most beneficial and pleasurable language-learning activities that there are. Even if you don't choose to read a lot in your own language, you will surprise yourself at how fun, challenging and rewarding you find reading in a foreign language to be.

Once you start feeling more confident about your language skills, you'll really start to see the benefits of reading. It will introduce you to essential vocabulary you might otherwise never have come across, and expose you to scenarios and situations that you would otherwise never be in.

To some extent it is necessary for you to already have a fairly advanced level in the language to get the most out of reading; however, even as a beginner there are ways to get started and already see the benefits.

Why Read?

There are four key reasons why reading is one of the most powerful language-learning techniques:

1. LEARNING FROM CONTEXT

Learning words in their natural context is one of the most powerful ways we have to learn more vocabulary, as we know from Chapter 4. However, the problem with this is that there can only be a limited number of natural contexts that we can ever physically be in at any one time.

What allows us to escape our surroundings and be placed somewhere totally new is reading. It's unlikely that you will ever spend a long time on a pre-revolution Tsarist Russian farm, but fortunately the descriptions in Tolstoy's books will take you there for you. Equally, a holiday in Germany does not normally involve a trip to the country's courts and mazes of bureaucracy, but reading Kafka can. As you become engrossed in the writing of the world's great authors, you will quickly absorb all sorts of new vocabulary that you might never have thought would be useful, but will surprise you at how much it comes in handy.

2. UNDERSTANDING CULTURE

Reading literature gives us an unparalleled insight into a different culture. Laid on the page before us are the immensely diverse ways in which people in different countries think. You will be able to get a sense of how much a book has influenced a national character, but also how much the national character has influenced the book.

In every country there are local literary 'greats' that everybody will have read, or at least pretend to have read, or at least pretend to have read, like Shakespeare, Camus or Goethe. You cannot really underestimate the extent to which these writers' works have shaped not only the culture, but also the language that is spoken in that country. Unbeknown even to many native speakers, such a large number of expressions, idioms and even names are direct quotations from these writers, and so it makes sense to understand and know these in the original.

3. READ REAL LANGUAGE

When you are reading a book designed for native speakers, you can be certain that the language used is genuine. This is your opportunity to cast aside your place as the 'learner' and engage with the language on the page as though you too were a native speaker. Of course it will be a challenge at first for you to follow it, but eventually it will give you such a sense of achievement when you are able to pick up a book, newspaper or magazine and read it as a native speaker would. Reading fiction is the best way to expose yourself and start absorbing the kind of language used for narration and humour that you will then be able to use in your own anecdotes and stories when talking to native speaker friends.

4. VIRTUAL IMMERSION

Reading books is by far the cheapest, fastest and easiest way to travel through space and time. When you are cut off from all other natural sources of the language, carrying a book around with you that you can open at any given moment and read a quick page from is an extremely powerful resource. You can be sitting on the bus in your town and suddenly find yourself surrounded by the great plains of Spain or dusty streets of North Africa, and most importantly have the entire thing narrated and described to you in the language of that country.

As you start to read for longer, more extended periods, you will find that you begin to enter a sort of immersion in the language. You will find yourself beginning to think and dream in it as though you were in the country. And you will begin to appreciate the beauty of the language you are learning, and the subtleties that can never be conveyed in translation.

What to Read?

The best thing to read is something you know you will enjoy. You should *want* to read it, and be interested in what the book is about, so you look forward to getting a chance to sit down with your book. It shouldn't necessarily always feel like a language-learning exercise. If you've picked the right book to read, you may become so engrossed that you don't always notice the large amount of language that you're learning as you go along.

However, sometimes the level that we have in the language we are learning means we can't always read what we want to read. When starting out with this as an exercise, it pays off to be slightly more strategic and read things that *are* suitable for your level, and that you will be able to get a lot out of.

Here are some suggestions:

★ PLAYS

Perhaps not your first thought when thinking about what to read in a foreign language, but there are a number of reasons why these are a good, logical place to start. Plays are written to be performed and therefore the language is written to be spoken. The dialogues that you read will be closer to the kind of spoken language you've been learning so far. Plays tend to be shorter than novels, which makes it easier for you to get through them quickly, and if you like you can also go back and re-read sections that you didn't understand the first time round.

★ SHORT STORIES

These require much less of a commitment than a whole novel, yet do offer you a chance to read longer passages of text. As these are so short it is easy to go back and re-read them multiple times after having looked up the vocabulary you didn't know, or even as an exercise to learn that vocabulary in the first place. Many short stories are also published in thematically related editions with other stories on the same theme, which means key vocabulary is very likely to be repeated and will be easier for you to learn. Plus, because these are so concise, you can quickly read through them and have the satisfaction of completing a story written entirely in a foreign language.

★ POEMS

Poems are very short pieces of writing that focus entirely on language. They play with different sounds, rhythms and rhymes, which often allows you to get a better idea of how a word should be pronounced than in a normal prose piece. More complicated poetry will require you to have a fairly advanced understanding of the language in order to truly understand it, but there are plenty of shorter pieces that are great for beginners too. Learning a poem off by heart is an excellent way to learn new words, grammar and practise your pronunciation.

★ NOVELS

These are probably the first thing that comes to mind when you think about reading. Novels are by far the most popular thing that people read around the world, and offer many benefits to language learners. They are generally quite lengthy, and will expose you to all sorts of different scenarios, descriptions and, of course, types of language. As the reader, you will become invested in finding out what happens at the end, which will spur you on to finish. However, unfortunately reading novels may be one of the hardest things for beginners to do. This is especially the case with the older classics that might have first got you interested in learning that language, as they are often written in older, more complicated language and will use plenty of vocabulary that you wouldn't encounter in everyday speech. It's great to aim to be able to read novels one day, but be aware that you will probably do better starting out with these shorter texts first.

★ **POPULAR FICTION**

Read what other people are reading. Modern novels usually have more up-to-date language and deal with topics that are current and that you might be able to relate to better. With recently published novels, there are often reviews or articles about them in national magazines or online which you could enjoy reading as a supplement. You're also more likely to be able to get hold of recently published novels in your own country, or online as an e-book.

★ **READ WHAT YOU KNOW**

Re-reading books you've already read in your own language means that you no longer have to focus so much on following the plot, as you already know what happens. You'll find yourself not needing to pause so often to look up a word, and you won't have to worry about missing important information for the plot, as you'll already know what happens in the end. That means you can just concentrate on understanding the language, and possibly even looking out for some differences in the translation too!

TOP TIP: READ THE SAME AUTHOR

If you find a book that you like, try to find others by the same author. Authors tend to write in a particular style and find themselves repeating phrases and expressions that they use in other books. That means you'll have a better chance of understanding a book by an author that you've already read than if you were to start getting used to a completely new author's style.

Common Challenges

Reading a book in a foreign language is one of the most rewarding things you can do as a language learner, but at first it can also be very frustrating. As adults, we are used to fluently and effortlessly being able to read whatever we need to. As learners of a new language, we have to go back almost right to the beginning. It takes longer for us to read each page, and there are plenty of words that we don't understand. Don't worry – this is completely normal, and as you get more practice, your reading will speed up!

The Four Reading Skills

When reading in our own language, we are constantly deploying four key reading skills that we develop from a young age. In a foreign language, we have to build these up once again:

1. SKIMMING

This is when we look quickly over a dense piece of text in order to get the gist of what's being said. We do this with emails, newspaper articles, reports, and usually anything we have to read but don't really want to.

2. SCANNING

We do this again with dense texts from which we need to extract specific pieces of information, for example: timetables, statistics and lists.

3. INTENSIVE

You probably have had the most practice of this in your foreign language, as this is what you are doing for every reading comprehension. You do this to analyse grammar structures and set out to learn new words.

4. EXTENSIVE

When you read a novel, you are reading extensively. You are not looking out for detail or paying much attention to individual words, you're happier just to read through without stopping, usually for pleasure. However, this skill can take the longest to develop with a foreign language, and so the other three are normally worked on first.

Setting Objectives and Milestones

Sometimes ploughing through a large book can feel like an impossible task in any language. In a foreign language, this feeling can be especially overwhelming.

It's important to have a sense of achievement with everything you do when learning a new language. If your only objective is to finish a book, it could be a very long time before you reach that point. Therefore, it makes sense to set yourself clear objectives each day, and milestones which you will feel happy when you reach.

OBJECTIVES

★ These can be quite simple, like reading a section without needing to look up a word. At first this may just be a paragraph, or even a sentence. Eventually, you can build this up to a page, ten pages, a chapter, or even the whole book!

★ Alternatively, you could make a note of how many new words you write down per page, and aim to reduce this number gradually as you read more.

★ Estimate a percentage of the text that you understand as you read through, e.g. 50 per cent on a first read. After you've looked up missing words, try to up this to 75 per cent or higher. When you feel you've reached 100 per cent understanding of a passage, you really have achieved something!

MILESTONES

★ Congratulate yourself every time you read a significant amount of the book. Every time you pass one of these milestones, you have made a big achievement. Typically you could think of this in terms of number of pages read: ten, twenty, fifty, one hundred, two hundred. You could also count chapters instead, depending on the book you're reading.

★ Each time you sit down with the book, keep a log of much you have read and how close you are to a particular milestone. This will motivate you to keep going.

TOP TIP: READ, RE-READ, AND RE-READ AGAIN

You are unlikely to understand everything the first time you read it. Therefore, don't be afraid to go back and re-read both the passages that you haven't understood, and also the ones that you have. Each time you are making those new words more memorable, and may notice things you didn't the first time around. Especially after you've looked up words, make sure you go back and read through to see how much more you understand now.

The 'Read with Your Eyes Shut' Technique

When you first start out reading in a foreign language, expect it to be fairly slow. Your eyes will be less used to instantly recognising words as they do in your native language, and you will constantly be encountering new words that you don't know, and pausing to look them up.

Don't allow these things to slow you down. Instead, simply ignore them. Don't pay attention to the words you don't know or don't recognise, and just keep reading until you've finished. This is called the 'read with your eyes shut' technique.

You won't understand an enormous amount of what's going on, but at the early stages it's crucial to read in this way for several reasons:

1. YOU WILL STILL GET THE GIST

Even if you can't understand every word, the more you read, the more you will start to pick up.

2. YOU WILL NOTICE WORDS COMING UP AGAIN AND AGAIN

That is a pretty reliable indication that you should learn that word.

3. YOU WILL BE READING LIKE YOU LISTEN

You can't pause things mid-conversation to reach for a dictionary, you just carry on and understand what you can. The same should go for reading, and you will find that eventually you've come across those words so many times that you can guess what they mean.

4. YOU WILL HAVE AN ENORMOUS SENSE OF ACHIEVEMENT

Each time you finish a story in a foreign language will feel like a victory. That's important for your morale, and ultimately will be what keeps bringing you back to reading.

When to Look Up Words

It's always a good idea to avoid looking up words as much as possible. Constantly reaching for a dictionary will distract you from what you're reading and you'll forget what you've just read. Plus, it's highly likely that after you've looked up the word in the dictionary you'll remember what it means in the context of the story, but forget what the original word was.

The point of reading in any language is to encounter new words. In our own language, though, we're more patient with ourselves. We form an idea of what a word means, without needing its exact definition. That's what we've been doing almost ever since we started reading as children. This is more of a challenge in a foreign language, because as adults we aren't used to not always understanding the full picture. But in the long term, it is necessary to get used to 'reading with your eyes shut' so that you can develop the reading skills you need for the language that you're learning.

However, there are two occasions when you *should* look up words in a dictionary.

1. **If a word appears five or more times in quick succession**. It probably is a word you should know. Most likely it will continue to reappear, so by the end of what you're reading you will probably have learnt it.

2. **If a word completely blocks the meaning of a sentence or paragraph that you're reading**. Then you have no choice but to look it up! If you've re-read it multiple times and are still none the wiser, you can reach for the dictionary with a clear conscience.

Whenever you do look up a word, there are two rules:

1. ALWAYS READ TO THE END OF THE SENTENCE FIRST

That way you don't get distracted, and may even be able to guess the meaning by then anyway.

2. ALWAYS RE-READ SECTIONS WHERE YOU'VE HAD TO LOOK UP WORDS

This helps to keep the new word in mind, and not just remember what it meant.

HOW TO SPEAK ANY LANGUAGE FLUENTLY

TOP TIP: WRITE WORDS DOWN!

Whenever you read anything in a foreign language, write new words and their meanings down on a separate pad of paper for you to review after you've finished reading.

SHOULD I WRITE IN BOOKS?

It might seem like a good idea to write translations of words above them in the text. However, the risk is that when you re-read them, your eyes will instantly be drawn to the translation that you've written in, and not the original word. The point of re-reading is to re-test yourself and see how many of those new words you've since learned. Therefore it's probably a better idea to make notes that you keep separate from the text.

Kindles and E-Books

This is by far the easiest and cheapest way to get hold of foreign language books. What's more, many devices have a 'touch to translate' feature, meaning that you can find out instantly what a word means, without having to spend time rooting through a physical dictionary.

If you pay attention to the rules about looking up words outlined above, an e-book with 'touch to translate' is an invaluable resource for any language learner. However, the ease of getting hold of translations so quickly means that you are even more likely to run the risk of not taking note of the new word that you should be learning.

Dual Translations and the 'Bilingual Book Bluff'

One of the most common tools for people to start reading in a foreign language is books that have dual translations. Those are books that have one page in the original language, and the other in the translation. The idea is that you can read both languages at the same time.

These books are great if all you really want to do is to read the book in translation, while occasionally dipping into the original. But if your aim is really to use these books to read and learn the original language, there are several reasons why you should be cautious of them:

★ YOU WILL JUST END UP READING THE TRANSLATION

The temptation is too great to be sure that you will always read in your target language.

★ IT TAKES AGES TO FIND THE WORD YOU'RE LOOKING FOR IN THE TRANSLATION

You can't look up a specific word. Instead, you have to re-read whole sections trying to find the one you're looking for.

★ TRANSLATIONS ARE UNRELIABLE

They are designed to be read as though they were originally written in that language, and so much of the meaning and nuance of the original words is lost.

★ IT'S LIKE DOING A SUDOKU WITH THE ANSWERS ON THE OPPOSITE PAGE

The point of reading in a foreign language is to challenge yourself. If you're only ever a glance away from finding out what everything means, you're less likely to try to solve the problems.

A Note on Translations

Translating is an extremely impressive and often undervalued skill. It allows us to read books written in languages we will never have the time to learn, as though they were written in our own language.

However, as all translators will tell you, it's almost impossible for a word in one language to mean exactly the same thing in another. When it comes to expressions, descriptions and idioms, those are even harder to explain literally without losing some or all of their meaning. Words and images can have entirely different connotations and implications in different cultures. Sometimes authors even write grammar mistakes into their characters' speech to provide more information about them and their background, which is almost impossible to translate accurately. For example, in Russian classic literature many of the characters mistakenly add 's' to the end of every word in order to sound more 'proper', but end up sounding like pretentious peasants. To a Russian audience this is hilarious, but to a foreign audience it is almost impossible to recreate this in translation, and as such very few translators ever do.

In translation, whole aspects of the story can be changed in order to make the text more readable for a foreign audience. That's not to say that the translation is necessarily wrong or 'unfaithful' to the original, but as a language learner it is something worth bearing in mind; especially if you are thinking of reading an original book alongside a translated version.

Translators often include a foreword to explain their choices and alert the reader to any stylistic decisions that have been taken in that edition. This is worth reading for reassurance if you find yourself lost between two seemingly entirely different versions of the same text.

Exercises

1. Read a whole chapter or short story in the language you are learning without looking up any vocabulary. Make a note of the words you don't know, and when you've finished look them up. Then re-read the chapter and see how much more you understand. Test yourself on these new words the next day and see how many you remember.

2. While reading a book, keep a notebook next to you and write a summary of each chapter you've read as you go along. Then compare your summaries to ones on websites like Wikipedia and Sparknotes to see whether you have fully understood all of the details.

3. Make a reading list of books you would like to read through in the language you are learning. Base this on recommendations from teachers or fellow students for books that they found were easy to read for your level, and also on your personal interests. Take great pleasure in working through this.

4. Work your way through the following reading milestones:

    a) Read a sentence with near 100% comprehension
    b) Read a paragraph with near 100% comprehension
    c) Read a page with near 100% comprehension
    d) Read a chapter with near 100% comprehension
    e) Read a book with near 100% comprehension

5. Try to find a film version in the target language of the book you are reading. As you complete each chapter, watch that section of the film. See if you notice any major differences, or if it helps clear up any confusions you had while reading.

HOW TO SPEAK ANY LANGUAGE FLUENTLY

Model Answers: Person H

1. At first, it is hard for Person H to stop reaching for the dictionary. He doesn't understand many words and loses concentration. However, he persists and just writes down words he doesn't know to look up later. Once he's looked them up, everything becomes clearer. As he reads through the text for a second time, he notices how much more he enjoys the story. The next day he tests himself on the vocabulary, and remembers the words' meanings through their association with the story. He then reads through the story for a third time and feels confident that many of those words are on the way to being learned.

2. Person H estimates he understands between 75–85% of the text. That's enough to follow the events, but with plenty to work on as well. Less than 75% understood is a struggle if he wanted to read a book and enjoy it. At 85% and above, he can almost read and enjoy it as though it were his native language.

3.

Author/Book	Notes
André Brink (anything)	Prominent Afrikaans author. Loud critic of Apartheid regime and post-Apartheid era. Colourful language and interesting content. Widely translated into English for comparison.
Fiela se Kind by Dalene Matthee	Old Afrikaans classic. Also a film version available.
Poetry by Ingrid Jonker	One of South Africa's greatest poets. Mentioned by Nelson Mandela in his inauguration speech as president in 1994. Many poems set to song.
Weerkaatsings by Eleanor Baker	Top five best-rated Afrikaans books on various websites.

Die Swerfjare van Poppie Nongena by Elsa Joubert	One of the most popular stories about apartheid in South Africa. Translated into thirteen languages and put on stage. Reviews describe it as 'untranslatable'.

4. Person H quickly finds a sentence that he understands fully. After a couple of weeks, he can get through a paragraph without the dictionary. It's a couple of months before he can do the same with a whole chapter. He understands the gist, but there are little words that spring up that he doesn't know. After nearly a year of reading, Person H can still not fully read a book and understand every word. He is getting better at resisting the dictionary, though, and is learning a lot of vocabulary as a result.

5. Person H watches the film version of *Fiela se Kind*. The film cuts some parts of the story, but it helps to see everything first. When reading, he can visualise some more difficult descriptions for which he might have lacked the vocabulary. He also re-watched sections of the films to recap on what he'd just read.

CHAPTER 9

Using Technology

The language-learning world is now awash with apps, websites, blogs and software that are all designed to help you learn a language. The days in which the only way to learn a language was with a book, a notepad and a pen are well and truly behind us.

Why Use Technology?

Technology has become an essential part of our lives. With internet usage rates as high as 92 per cent for young people in the United States, using technology is how we spend a significant portion of our lives.

To set up a successful language-learning routine, technology can be the perfect solution. If you are a regular smartphone or social media user anyway, these provide the perfect way for you to make language learning a part of your life, without causing you to unsustainably disrupt your routine.

If you're an auditory or visual learner, technology can offer the visual stimulation and interaction that you need to learn a language, in a way that books never can.

As you will see over the course of this chapter, the internet is brimming with resources that will revolutionise the way in which you learn languages, so long as you are confident that you know how to use them.

Spaced Repetition Software

Spaced Repetition Software has revolutionised the way we learn vocabulary, and is now at the heart of many of the most successful language-learning courses, websites and apps on the market. It is now easier to learn words and really remember them in the long term than ever before.

Spaced Repetition Software (or S.R.S.) operates on the basis that the brain can remember things more easily if it is exposed to them repeatedly, at regular intervals. This is the same way of thinking that leads to the advice in Chapter 2 that short and intensive bursts of study are much more effective than studying for hours at a time. However, S.R.S. goes one step further by calculating how often you need to revisit a piece of vocabulary in order to learn it and determining which words need more attention and which need less.

Many of the apps mentioned in this chapter use variations of Spaced Repetition Software, notably Memrise, Duolingo and Anki. It is wholly recommended that you experiment with them and include these as part of your routine.

Top Language-Learning Apps

These resources are the most popular at the time of writing according to usage and reviews worldwide. Free ones are marked (F) and paid ones are marked (P).

★ DUOLINGO (F) – WWW.DUOLINGO.COM

Duolingo is by far the most popular language-learning site, probably owing to the fact that it is completely free and extremely user-friendly. Its courses will allow you to make excellent headway in the language you're learning, so that you can start holding basic conversations and learn by using. Duolingo rewards you with points and maintains a leader board to keep you motivated, which makes learning a new language feel like a game.

★ BABBEL (P) – WWW.BABBEL.COM

Babbel is one of the largest language-learning sites out there, with over twenty million users in more than 190 countries. Babbel offers courses in Dutch, Danish, English, French, German, Indonesian, Italian, Norwegian, Portuguese, Russian, Swedish, Spanish and Turkish, and is available for a small monthly subscription. Babbel gradually builds up your vocabulary with audio and visuals, while including short but clear grammar explanations when needed.

★ MEMRISE (F/P) – WWW.MEMRISE.COM

Memrise was co-founded by Memory Grandmaster Ed Cooke and it mainly helps you to learn vocabulary. It encourages you to think about mnemonics for words you're struggling to learn, and even allows you to create your own memes by uploading your own photos or using ones from the internet. Memrise uses Spaced Repetition Software to determine how often you should review the words you're learning, and will send you friendly reminders on your phone or by email. There are courses for almost every language at different levels available, but you are also free to upload your own. Many courses match up with textbooks and course books, which makes Memrise a good companion for learning vocabulary, no matter which way you approach learning the language.

★ ROSETTA STONE (P) – WWW.ROSETTASTONE.COM

Rosetta Stone is the oldest language-learning software around. Thanks to its heavy advertising campaign, it's also perhaps the most well known. It works similarly to Babbel in using pictures and audio to teach vocabulary. Its main difference, however, is that it deliberately avoids any use of English, and prides itself on not teaching any grammar at all. It also uses complex speech recognition technology to give you some speaking practice. Many home users will find Rosetta Stone prohibitively expensive, costing upwards of eighty pounds for a single level. Many reviewers also find the grammar-free approach frustrating, which means that despite its reputation, Rosetta Stone is one of the least popular language-learning tools for reviewers on the internet.

★ BUSUU (P) – WWW.BUSUU.COM

Busuu combines courses with an online community, offering you both the chance to learn a language and practise it with native speakers using forums and live chat. You can also upload things you've written or recordings of you speaking for native speakers to give you feedback. This could be a great solution for people working without a teacher, and it certainly works out a lot cheaper to pay a monthly subscription rather than pay for somebody's time by the hour. There is a free version of Busuu too, but this comes without access to the online community.

★ YABLA (P) – WWW.YABLA.COM

Yabla offers fun and interesting videos in French, German, Spanish, Italian, English and Chinese for learners of different levels. The content is generally interesting and relevant for anybody who wants to find out about a country's culture, as well as learning its language, and videos come with bilingual subtitles that allow you to read both the English and the original, while also listening along. There are also interactive games that make you fill in missing words and answer questions about the videos to make sure you really pay attention!

★ FLUENTU (P) – WWW.FLUENTU.COM

FluentU takes real videos in French, German, Spanish, English, Chinese and Japanese from TV shows and YouTube and you can turn on bilingual subtitles to allow you to read along and learn from them. All videos are categorised by level, making it easier for you to find ones that are suitable for you. You can hover your mouse over words you don't know to get an instant translation. FluentU will also compile flashcards for you from the words you didn't know.

★ ANKIAPP (F) – WWW.ANKIAPP.COM

Anki is another app that uses Spaced Repetition Software to help you learn vocabulary with digital flashcards. The system is slightly more complicated to set up than Memrise, but once you get to grips with it, it can be easily customised and suited to your own purposes. It is also more straightforward to use Anki when learning languages with different scripts such as Arabic or Farsi, and also for including important grammar information for more complex languages. It has a much plainer interface which may appeal less to visual learners.

★ MINDSNACKS (F/P) – WWW.MINDSNACKS.COM

Mindsnacks is aimed primarily at children and adults who love playing games. It has many language-related games that will teach you vocabulary and grammar in eight different languages. If you want to have fun while learning languages with interactive and addictive games, this is a great place to start!

Eight Free Websites to Help Learn Languages

Apart from the paid options, many valuable resources are available on the internet for completely free. Below are eight of the best and most useful tools, and some tips on how you can get the most out of them.

★ READLANG – WWW.READLANG.COM

Readlang is not technically a website, but actually a plug-in that you can easily install on your internet browser. It enables you to click and have an instant translation of any word, on any website you visit, in any language. Readlang will also store a list of the words you look up, so you can review them and make sure that you learn them.

★ GOOGLE – WWW.GOOGLE.COM

The world's largest search engine can be an excellent way to double-check spellings of words, and whether or not certain expressions exist in the first place. If you have a gut feeling that needs double-checking, this is a fast and accurate way to do it as it will show you all of the instances in which that expression has been used. If few results are found, that means that expression probably doesn't exist.

★ GOOGLE TRANSLATE – HTTP://TRANSLATE.GOOGLE.COM

Google Translate is infamous for its mistranslations and mistakes, and so it should never be used in isolation or in place of a reliable dictionary or source of language. However, if you are writing letters or essays in a foreign language, translating it back into your native language is an excellent way to check for spelling errors and other possible mistakes.

★ GOOGLE IMAGES – WWW.GOOGLE.COM/IMAGES

Visual learners can really benefit from this one. If you're in need of a visual aid to go along with a new word that you're learning, simply search for a picture of that word in the language you are learning. This will give you the chance to see it in an authentic cultural context, and will be great for creating memes or flashcards.

★ LANG-8 – WWW.LANG-8.COM

Lang-8 is an online community similar to Busuu, but free and without specifically designed courses. It allows you to interact with native speakers in order to receive feedback and corrections on things that you've written or recorded for free, on the understanding that you will return the favour.

★ PONS – WWW.PONS.EU

Pons is one of the largest and most comprehensive online dictionaries available for free. It provides more than just the translation, as it gives useful information for understanding the context in which a word should be used, and any nuances that go along with it.

★ GLOSBE – WWW.GLOSBE.COM

Glosbe is like an online dictionary, but its selling point is that it will search through published translations to find the words you're looking for, and display them for you in the context that they have been used. This means you can read a whole paragraph in your native language and the target language and decide for yourself whether or not the word you've been suggested is really the word you need.

★ WORDREFERENCE – WWW.WORDREFERENCE.COM

Wordreference is a huge online dictionary offered in many languages. It is not as thorough as Pons, but its main advantage is the expansive and thorough forums used by its users to ask specific questions about grammar, vocabulary and usage which will help you to know whether you're learning to use a particular word correctly, or identify any mistakes.

Social Media

There are 2.2 billion social media users worldwide at the time of writing. In the United States, as much as 78 per cent of the population use social networks. Sites like Facebook, Twitter, Instagram and Pinterest are increasingly where we are spending time, using computers and smartphones in almost every area of our lives.

Although social media has also been blamed for increasing levels of procrastination and lowering worker productivity on an unprecedented scale, if used correctly it can be an extremely valuable and easily accessible tool to help you with your language learning. The fact that we spend so much time on it is precisely what makes it so useful.

Customise Your Feed

You may not remember ever asking to be shown endless photos of cats and people's breakfast, but you actually have far more influence over your news feeds than you might think. Facebook's algorithms will show you more of the things you tell it that you like, and fewer of the things that you hide or unfollow. Therefore, if you're able to increase the amount of language-related stories appearing there, that means every time you check Facebook you are gaining more exposure to language and creating more opportunities to learn:

★ LIKE LANGUAGE-LEARNING PAGES
Especially ones that post a 'word of the day' or anything similar.

★ LIKE NEWS/BLOG PAGES IN YOUR TARGET LANGUAGE
Even if you just read the headlines rather than the whole article, that is good practice and you will feel yourself improving. Don't forget to read the 'Comments' section, too! These are usually written in much more straightforward language and can be quite entertaining.

★ FRIENDS FROM OTHER COUNTRIES
Read their posts and statuses. This is great for learning the real language that people use in their daily lives.

Hashtag Hacks
One of the best advantages of using social media is that it gives us a chance to see real language in action. That means you are always just a few clicks away from being able to prove to yourself that the language you are learning really is the language people speak. When you learn vocabulary, you can use it to see exactly when and how different words are used and in which contexts.

A fun and useful exercise on Twitter or Instagram is to search for hashtags of words you are learning and read the various tweets and pictures that use them. This works perhaps best for abstract concepts, as they are likely to show up the most surprising and interesting results.

For example, searching the German word 'Ferien' will show you lots of pictures of people's holidays in exotic places. If you search 'zufrieden' though, which means 'satisfied', you will see pictures of people's achievements, their facial expressions, weight-loss photos and other invaluable memory aids that will give context and meaning to the vocabulary you're learning.

Language-Learning Groups

There are so many people on social media learning languages, and a wealth of supportive and useful groups that connect them. In these groups you can ask specific questions that you have, but also see questions from other people that can be useful, and fill your wall with inspirational stories and photos that will remind you to keep up your language learning.

These groups can also be a good way to meet people interested in learning foreign languages, as well as native speakers who might offer lessons or be interested in setting up a language exchange with you.

Online Community

Many people find it best to share their learning with other people who can keep them motivated to continue striving towards their goals. When it comes to something as specific as language learning, though, you probably don't know that many people who share your enthusiasm.

Fortunately, the internet has brought many people with the same interests together and there is now a growing community of people online who encourage and help each other to learn languages. Many of these people communicate with each other via Facebook and other social media sites, but also upload videos to YouTube and write on forums about their language-learning progress.

The online language-learning community is increasingly coming offline as well, with yearly events such as the Polyglot Conference organised to bring lovers of language together. This allows them to make friends, and also hear talks and lectures on a range of subjects relating to language learning.

Why You Shouldn't Use Technology

Many people swear by the apps they use, and many companies market their products as though you wouldn't be able to learn a language without them. There are, however, some reasons why technology might not be the be-all and end-all of learning a new language.

★ CLICK, CLICK, CLICK

When we write things by hand, we develop a **muscle memory** of what we have written. When we click on the correct answer on our screen, we don't. You are more likely to remember things you write by hand than things that you type, so always keep an old-fashioned pad of paper and a pen with you whenever learning languages.

★ ONLINE RESOURCES ARE HARDER TO CUSTOMISE

If you like underlining, highlighting, making notes and doodling in the margins, then you will find learning from a computer very restrictive and frustrating. When you type up notes, you are restricted by your own word processing skills as to whether or not you can truly make them 'yours'.

★ DO YOU STILL WANT TO BE STARING AT A SCREEN?

If you spend most of your day working on a computer or tablet, the last thing you want to be doing in your free time is spending more time with a screen. Plus, as with all technology, it can be hard to really focus on the task at hand, as you can be subconsciously reminded of all the other things you could be doing that are just a few clicks away.

★ DON'T GET TRAPPED INTO A SUBSCRIPTION

Apps are designed to keep you coming back and using them, regardless of whether or not it might be time to try something new. If you have a monthly subscription, it can be easy to forget about it and find yourself paying for a product you're no longer using, and no longer need. Set yourself reminders and keep on top of what you've signed up for!

Virtual Immersion

Many people go abroad to learn a language because it gives them an opportunity to be completely surrounded by it, and the chance to use it every day. Unfortunately, though, with jobs, families, and lives set up at home, few of us are at liberty to do something so drastic.

However, many of the benefits of being abroad in an immersed environment can be recreated virtually with the help of the internet at home. As so much live radio and TV from other countries can now be accessed online, this allows you to tune in whenever you want.

Identify at which points in your existing routine you listen to the radio, watch TV, read books, read newspapers, or have any contact with your native language, and replace these sources with ones from the language you are learning. Allow yourself to be in constant contact with the language, just as you would if you were abroad, even if it is only in the background.

Gradually you will notice that it feels more natural to switch to speaking the language you're learning, and you will be able to recall words and phrases much more easily than before. When you come to learn new words, some may already seem more familiar, as you may have heard them being used without realising it.

Exercises

1. Every week try out one of the resources listed in the previous chapter. Which do you prefer for:

   a) Vocabulary

   b) Grammar

   c) Pronunciation

   d) Reading/Listening practice

   e) Overall fun

2. Experiment for a whole week using just technology for your language study. What differences do you notice compared to learning on paper in terms of:

   c) Retention of material

   d) Ability to concentrate for longer

   e) Engagement with the material

   f) Ease of access

3. Take a list of vocabulary from your textbook and search each of the words in Google Images. Save one picture that you like best for each word onto your computer in a folder with the title of the list you are learning. Later when you test yourself, look through these pictures without using the English to see which ones you remember.

4. On Instagram or Twitter, browse hashtags of a new word that you have learned. Look at the other photos and tweets that come up, and see what new vocabulary you find that is related. If you notice words re-occurring, try to learn these as well.

5. Search for groups on Facebook for the language that you are learning. Investigate them, and choose which ones you'd like to join. Think about:

a) The quality of responses people get when they ask a question

b) The relevance of questions being asked

c) The friendliness and helpfulness of other members

d) The group's size (between a thousand and ten thousand members is ideal)

Model Answers: Person I

1. Person I lives a busy life. He likes using apps, and finds Memrise to be the best for vocabulary. He likes Duolingo but thinks Babbel tends has the clearest grammar explanations, and likes the voice recognition function for practising vocabulary. In the evenings he'll sit and read an article on BBC Brasil with Readlang, and finds Yabla videos the most fun.

2. Person I finds he works best when using technology in tandem with traditional methods. For longer study periods, he prefers to sit with a textbook and shut himself away from other distractions. Technology really comes in handy for his revision sessions, while apps and podcasts present an easy way to access the language while on the go.

3. Person I finds lots of images that he likes, so saves many into a Powerpoint presentation that he watches on his phone. When he can't remember a word, he goes back to look through the images again to find new ones that he likes better.

4. Looking through #verão (summer), Person I finds lots of related words, like #praia (beach), #sol (sun) and #descanso (rest). After a while, he has put together a whole vocabulary list of summer-related words.

5. There are lots of Portuguese groups on Facebook to join. Some of these are more linguistics-orientated, and others seem to just be photos of Brazil with no language element. He finds one called 'Portuguese-English Exchange', where Brazilians write questions in English and vice versa.

HOW TO SPEAK ANY LANGUAGE FLUENTLY

CHAPTER 10

Sounding Less 'Foreign'

You can have studied all the grammar in the world, and have a vocabulary stretching as far as the eye can see. But there is still something that gives you away, and it's not necessarily your accent.

Why Do You Sound Foreign?

Even though what you're saying makes sense and everybody understands you, you still sound foreign. That's because there is something missing. Technically your language is correct, but it still doesn't sound authentic.

Most of the time the reason why this happens is because people first decide what they'd like to say in their native language, and then try and translate that into the language they are speaking. Again, that's not to say that the words they're using aren't correct. It's just that no native speaker would ever say it quite in that way.

It's precisely at this point that language learning moves away from the nitty-gritty of techniques, technology and determination, and moves into a slightly more abstract sphere. This stage is about identity, culture and establishing your relationship with those things in a foreign language, as a foreigner.

The instincts that you have from your native language may clash with the ones you're developing in your new one. This can cause you to make mistakes in your grammar, and as a worst case scenario, be misunderstood.

If you've wondered why so many non-native English speakers say 'the informations', 'I've arrived to the airport', or 'I have spoken with her yesterday', there are several reasons why. In many other European languages these are all perfectly natural things to say. In French: 'les informations', 'je suis arrivé à l'aéroport', and 'j'ai parlé avec elle hier' are all grammatically correct. Indeed, many non-Anglophone businessmen, politicians and journalists live their whole lives speaking English without correcting these and never really encounter any problems.

But if you identify these errors and fix them, you suddenly have a chance to go above and beyond the glass ceiling that your average non-native speaker will keep hitting. If you can master sounding less foreign, it certainly won't go unnoticed.

What Is an Idiom?

An idiom is a natural part of speech that, when you stop to think about it, makes no sense whatsoever. 'It's raining cats and dogs', 'swings and roundabouts', and 'it's all gone pear-shaped' are all examples of idioms that are so vivid in meaning to native English speakers, but are initially nonsensical to anybody else. To understand an idiom, you have to be a member of the club that uses them. If you want in on that club, the very first thing you need to do is start learning these.

Through learning idioms, you will discover a fantastic way

to understand more about a different culture. Idioms are in themselves a product of culture, and so they carry enormous cultural and emotional baggage with them. One example is that in Russian it is not Rome, but Moscow that was 'built in a day': Москва в один день не строилась. Another is that in Greek when somebody is sitting around doing nothing, they are 'swatting flies': βαράει μύγες.

When you first come across one of these idioms it will sound bizarre, and it may even seem unbelievable to you that people use them at all. But as idioms are such a crucial, fundamental part of language, so many people use them without even realising it. If somebody starts using them around you, that is a sign that the person you're speaking to is relaxed, feels comfortable with you, and respects your level in their language enough to assume that you'll understand.

Take it as a compliment, don't feel ashamed to ask what it means, and see if you can find an opportunity to start using them yourself.

Why Do People Use Idioms?

Idioms are like a splash of colour on the canvas of language. The point of them is to take you out of the situation you're in, and compare it to a situation with a clear and unequivocal outcome. Idioms are a like an easy and comprehensible way to make sense of the many bizarre things that can happen in life, and to help you see what you should do about them.

Many idioms are visually striking and even humorous. Many native speakers are deliberately creative with the idioms that they use, coming up with their own or relying on wordplay and puns to customise them and make them their own. This, however, can complicate matters somewhat for you as the learner. Most people are sympathetic to the fact that idioms can be confusing for foreigners, and so will tone their use of them down when speaking to you. Often older speakers, or those that have had little contact with foreigners, will not always be fully aware of how the way in which they speak makes it harder for you to understand, and so these conversations will require more effort on your part.

As a foreigner, successfully deploying an idiom in a foreign language during natural conversation is like winning a medal at the Olympics. You will be sure to impress whoever you're speaking with, and they will really appreciate the time you have put in to learn about their culture and the way in which people speak.

That's assuming that you use the right idiom at the right time, of course.

Eccentric Expressions from Around the World

★ **PORTUGUESE: ALIMENTAR UM BURRO COM PÃO DE LÓ**
Translation: **To feed a donkey sponge cake**
Ever been really nice to somebody who wasn't nice back, or definitely didn't deserve it? Put that sponge cake away!

★ **DUTCH: IETS VOOR EEN APPEL EN EEN EI KOPEN**
Translation: **To buy something for an apple and an egg**
Did the car salesman see you coming that morning and flog you the extra Sat-Nav, sunroof and glow-in-the-dark wheels for a hefty extra sum? You just paid with an apple and an egg!

★ **GERMAN: TOMATEN AUF DEN AUGEN HABEN**
Translation: **To have tomatoes on your eyes**

When all your friends are telling you you're making the wrong decision but you just can't see it yourself. There's something they see that you don't. But that's not your fault, because in German you have tomatoes on your eyes, making you blind.

★ POLISH: NIE MÓJ CYRK, NIE MOJE MAŁPY
Translation: **Not my circus, not my monkeys**
Everything's gone wrong. You've missed your flight, lost your passport, run out of money and you're trying to persuade the taxi driver at the airport to take you to the nearest hotel. He shrugs, and tells you it's not his circus, and certainly not his monkeys.

★ FINNISH: PÄÄSTÄÄ SAMMAKKO SUUSTA
Translation: **To let the frog out of your mouth**
You say something and the room falls silent. Everyone looks at you in horror. Why, of all things, did you say that? The frog you just let out of your mouth starts hopping away.

★ **RUSSIAN: EXATЬ ЗAЙЦEM**

Translation: **To travel on the back of the hare**

In Russian travelling on the back of the hare means getting a free ride. Getting on the metro without a ticket is like a tortoise travelling on the back of a hare. And you will get fined.

★ **FRENCH: LE DÉMON DE MIDI**

Translation: **The midday devil**

If you've got the midday devil, it means you're at that point in your life when you are consumed by existential angst. The famous midlife crisis is upon you.

★ **HUNGARIAN: MIÉRT ITATOD AZ EGEREKET?**

Translation: **Why are you giving milk to the mice?**

This little question is what Hungarian children are asked when they cry. Their tears are like milk for the mice who come and drink them afterwards. If you want to keep the mice away, you have to dry your eyes.

★ **SPANISH: MÁS SANO QUE UNA MANZANA**

Translation: **Healthier than an apple**

What do you mean I should take it easy? I'm healthier than an apple at the moment! Never felt fitter in my life.

★ **GREEK: ΑΠ' ΤΗΝ ΠΟΛΗ ΕΡΧΟΜΑΙ ΚΑΙ ΣΤΗΝ ΚΟΡΥΦΗ ΚΑΝΕΛΑ**

Translation: **I come from the city and on the mountain top is cinnamon**

Come again? This bizarre expression is deployed to point out when someone is being completely inconsistent and making no sense. Because responding to nonsense with nonsense leads to more sense. Right?

Learning Idioms

As you can see from the examples we've just had, almost anything and everything could be an idiom. There really is no way to predict these or second-guess them. You just have to learn them.

Native speakers learn these idioms through a lifetime of speaking the language with their family, friends and compatriots. They pick and choose the ones they want to use, but will generally have some idea what even the ones they don't mean.

As a foreigner, you don't have the luxury of a lifetime to pick these up, but there are shortcuts.

Apart from dictionaries, make an effort to listen out for these expressions every time you come into contact with the language. Make a mental (or physical) note of them, and also consider the following:

★ PROFILE

Who used the expression? What do you know about their background? Is the expression they're using linked to any specific political views? It helps to have as much information as you can get.

★ CONTEXT

What was the point that the idiom was trying to make? Was it used in a friendly way? What emotions accompanied it?

★ REACTION

If speaking to another native speaker, how did they react? Did they laugh? Were they horrified? Did they not respond at all? This tells you the kind of reaction you might get if you used the same expression.

As already mentioned, these expressions carry lots of emotional baggage and attachments. Until you develop as profound an understanding as you can about what an idiom means and how it can be used, be cautious of using them, for fear of letting the frog out of your mouth.

Humour in Foreign Languages

Jokes don't tend to work in other languages. They rarely survive the translation process. That is because the language in which a joke is told is vital for its success.

Humour as a more general concept, however, might be slightly easier to explain. Broadly speaking, humour is always different in different countries. Almost every culture will think that they are the funniest, and they'll often see other cultures' jokes as utterly humourless.

There are two big milestones that every language learner will cherish. The first is that moment when you understand a joke in your new language. It could be the worst joke in the world, and if you'd heard it in your native language you wouldn't have even turned your nose up at it. But because it marks the culmination of so much work and the acquisition of so much cultural knowledge, you can be sure that you will find it far funnier than you ever would normally. Expect to guffaw, and react more than anybody else in the room. And you should, because you have just achieved something very special.

The second milestone is when you make a joke yourself. This time, it'll be the people around you who'll be in stitches. They will be delighted that finally their foreign-sounding friend who's always mixing up words and apologising for not being able to say what they mean can actually be funny too. When you've reached this point, you can feel well and truly pleased with yourself.

TOP TIP: WATCH STAND-UP COMEDY

If you want to find out what makes the people who speak your new language laugh, watch their comedy. Stand-up exists in some form or another in nearly every country in the world, and YouTube is full of clips for you to watch. Find some comedians that you like and watch what you can find of their shows. If you're really lucky and you stumble upon someone very popular, you may even find a video of their routine with subtitles. Listen out for wordplay, expressions, puns, and think about what kind of thing forms the subjects of their jokes. Take notes, and if you know any native speakers ask them what they think of the jokes. Comedy is a goldmine for understanding different cultures.

Appreciating Cultural Sensitivities

Speaking a new language comes with plenty of responsibility. You should always make yourself aware of the do's and don'ts of wherever your chosen language is spoken. Every culture has a set of unwritten rules. There are things you don't say, things you don't do, and things you never ask for or about. While many of these rules might be common to lots of different cultures, there are plenty more that you will never have heard of, and certainly would never have thought about.

In many countries in the world, there are some subjects that are entirely unacceptable as jokes, or even idioms. In the English-speaking world, for example, it is completely taboo to make reference to race, gender, sexuality or disability in jokes. This is also true in many other countries around the world, but not to the same degree everywhere, and as a result you may hear people saying things that you might be quite horrified to hear at home. As a rule of thumb, you should never say or do anything that makes you feel uncomfortable in a foreign culture, but you should also be aware that you cannot react in exactly the same way that you would at home. Many people simply may never have thought about the meaning of what they're saying, and will probably not mean any offence by it.

Restraint is also advised when using vulgar language. As with all idiomatic expressions, swearing often carries connotations and conforms to an etiquette that will be unfamiliar to you as a foreigner. By all means, it can be useful to know what such words mean, but that does not give you the right to use them yourself.

Thinking in a Foreign Language

This is arguably one of the biggest challenges, but also one of the biggest rewards of learning a new language. Finding yourself thinking in a foreign language without realising it is a real achievement. It compares only to that special moment when you suddenly realise you've been dreaming in the language too. These things help to make it feel as though the language has become part of your identity, and make the thought of one day feeling fluent draw ever closer.

It's easiest to think in the language after you've spent extended periods of time immersed in it, having only been listening to that language and little else. After a while, it will gradually start to replace your native language as your default for when you need to refer to certain things around you. If you spend some time living with a host family, one of the most common things to switch over to the new language are topics to do with the house, the kitchen and mealtimes. You will find

HOW TO SPEAK ANY LANGUAGE FLUENTLY

that these words in your new language develop extra connotations and trigger memories of your time in immersion, far more so than the words for them in your native language.

If you re-enter immersion after a period of time spent outside of it, you will eventually experience a 'click' moment, when you find yourself remembering words you don't fully remember ever learning. This is because you will have developed connotations and connections to the words you know that lead you to remember other words that you didn't know so well. Simply the fact that you're having so much contact with the language is what allows this to happen, which is something you might never have achieved if you'd just continued to speak your own language all the time.

An excellent activity to fill your 'dead time' (see Chapter 2) is to set yourself the task of thinking in the foreign language. For example, next time you take the bus try thinking in the foreign language until you get off. Just think your normal thoughts, looking around yourself for inspiration if you like, and see how easily it comes to you. Find alternatives for words you don't know, and make a mental note of the words you'd like to look up later when you get the chance. Do this as often as you can, and get into the habit of using the language at all times.

The number one rule of this, however, is that translation is prohibited. In other words, don't think a sentence in your native language and then try to convert it into the foreign language. You will run the risk of sounding foreign or unnatural, and ultimately that will slow down your fluency. Train yourself to see an object and immediately think of the word in the foreign language first. The more you practise this, the easier it will become and the more fluent you will feel and sound.

Exercises

1. Listen to a native speaker of the language you are learning speaking your language. What mistakes do they make? Write them down and see if you can work out what is causing them to make that mistake. Here are some potential causes:

    a) A false friend in their language
    b) A mix-up in grammar
    c) Misuse of an expression or idiom

2. Think about the expressions and idioms you use in your own language, and keep a tally of the most popular ones you use in any given week. Find ways to translate these or equivalents in the language you are learning. Try to use as many of these in your next conversation with your teacher or language exchange partner.

3. Learn five popular jokes in the language you are learning. Ask yourself:

    a) Do you find these funny?
    b) Why are they considered funny in the culture of the language you are learning?
    c) Are there equivalent jokes to these in your culture?
    d) Which new words did you need to learn for these jokes?

4. Create a virtual immersion environment in the language you are learning for twenty-four hours. In that time everything you hear, everything you read and all conversations you have should be in the target language. How easier or harder does this make it for you to think in your target language?

5. Next time you see your language exchange partner or teacher, ask them to make a note of everything you say that sounds particularly foreign or unnatural, but that still could make sense. See if you can find ways to make what you're trying to say sound more authentic. Try to spot recurring patterns.

Model Answers: Person J

1. Person J listens to her Greek friend speaking English and notices some recurring errors. Instead of: 'Do you think that ...?' she says 'Do you say that ...?' This is because, in Greek, the verb 'to say' is commonly used for making suggestions. Also, instead of: 'Are you thinking of going on holiday?', she says 'thinking <u>to</u> go'. That is because, in Greek, you just need 'to think' + the verb for this construction.

2. 'Best of both worlds', 'The benefit of the doubt', 'Keep something at bay', 'On the ball', 'Wouldn't be caught dead'.

3. Greek humour is very different to English humour, and seems to be focused much more on things that are visually funny or slap-stick. Person J discovers Greeks often see the funny side of life and make jokes about themselves too. She is careful to be respectful when making those kinds of jokes herself.

4. Person J replaces as many of her daily activities with Greek ones as she can. She listens to Greek radio in the morning instead of the BBC, she reads Greek news on her phone on the way to work, and at her desk she listens to Greek radio again with earphones. In the evenings, instead of English TV she watches Greek TV, and she schedules in some extra Skype lessons with her teacher. She can't completely cut English out of her life, but she replaces it as much as possible. This is tiring to maintain for more than a week, but she notices that she remembers words more quickly, and even finds her thoughts drifting into Greek every now and then.

5. Person J's biggest problem is overusing certain words. Instead of just saying 'I think that ...', her conversation partner suggests she uses 'I believe', 'it seems', 'I've got the impression' and some other alternatives. There are also times when she uses the wrong preposition because it would sound right in English but not in Greek.

CHAPTER 11

Taking Tests and Getting Certificates

Many people who learn languages choose to do so with the specific aim in mind of ultimately taking an exam. This is certainly true for anybody studying a language at school or university, but also for many non-students who simply wish to gain a qualification in the language they are learning.

Why Take Exams?

There are a number of reasons why taking exams might be a good idea:

★ HAVE SOMETHING TO AIM FOR

Paying the enrolment fee and writing the date in your calendar means that skipping study time is now no longer an option. With every hour that passes, exam day draws closer and with it the possibility of a result that you would not be happy with. Setting yourself deadlines is an excellent way to focus your learning, and as exams are non-negotiable, this makes them very good deadlines.

★ PROVE YOUR SKILLS

Many people learn languages in order to improve their CV and job prospects. But without a certificate to back up your claims, prospective employers have no evidence to suggest that you really can speak the language. Being able to produce a certificate that proves how well you can speak the language instantly solves that problem.

★ OBJECTIVE ASSESSMENT

Your good friends will always tell you how well you speak their language, but after a point, you'll start looking for slightly more reassurance than that. Taking an exam offers you the chance to get an objective analysis of how well you really are doing, and a good idea of which areas you should be working on in order to move forwards.

Know Your Level

Every stage of your language-learning journey will bring you fresh challenges. The best way to approach these is to understand and anticipate them. That way you can tackle them head on.

If you take a test and work within the framework of the different 'levels' of language learning, that will make you aware of the kinds of challenges that you face. It will also spell out for you where your weak areas are, and what you could do in the meantime to fill the gaps that this has left.

Knowing your level is about planning. When you plan, you can arrange to use materials that are suitable for you and will help you, rather than ones that are too hard or too easy.

The Common European Framework of Reference

The most commonly used system of ranking language ability around the world is called the Common European Framework of Reference. This was created by the European Commission after 20 years of research into language learning and education. It is still the only system officially recognised by the European Union, and is widely used around the world. By familiarising yourself with this scale, employers across Europe and the rest of the world will be able to gauge whether the level you have is suitable for the job they are offering.

A1: Elementary	A2: Advanced Beginner
You can interact in a simple way, ask and answer simple questions, and talk about very familiar topics or ones of immediate need. You will have a basic idea of grammar and different tenses, and should get by as a tourist in most situations.	You can begin to function in social situations, handle short exchanges, discuss plans, make and respond to invitations and offers, and handle basic transactions in shops, post offices and banks. You will have a more in depth idea of grammar, and will more than cope as a tourist.
B1: Pre-Intermediate	**B2: Upper Intermediate**
You can maintain conversations, express yourself in a range of contexts, and follow the main points of extended discussion around you. It may still take you longer to make your point, but you can make it comprehensibly. You can cope flexibly with problems in everyday life that are outside of your routine, and enter unprepared into conversations on familiar topics.	You can effectively hold your own in a debate or argument. You can explain and sustain your opinion in discussions using explanations, reasons and comments. You can understand in detail what is said to you in spoken language, and interact with a degree of fluency and spontaneity, without putting strain on the conversation. You are very aware of mistakes and increasingly are able to correct them as you make them.

C1: Advanced	C2: Mastery
You have a wide vocabulary which allows you to have fluent, spontaneous and almost effortless communication. You can talk around vocabulary gaps by using the words you do know, and no longer need to search for expressions or words as often. Only conceptually difficult conversation topics cause problems. Your speech is clear, smooth-flowing, well-structured and shows controlled use of organisational patterns, connectors and cohesive devices.	You demonstrate a degree of precision, appropriateness and ease with the language. You can convey finer shades of meaning by using a range of different vocabulary, all with good accuracy. You have a good command of idioms, expressions and colloquialisms. You can backtrack and work around a difficulty so smoothly that whoever you're speaking to will hardly notice it.

If you're not sure which of these descriptions best matches your level, there are many free tests you can do online. When signing up for a language course, you will also be asked to complete a written and spoken assessment of your level to ensure your suitability for the course.

Tailor Your Learning to Your Level

As soon as you have worked out which level you are at already and which level you'd like to work towards, you can immediately start planning your learning. You can adjust everything you're doing to make it fit better with your needs and objectives.

The first thing to do is make sure that the materials you are using are correct for your level. Note that the level advertised on the front cover will always refer to the level you are working towards by the end of the course, not the level that you are to start with. If you are at an A2 level currently, you should be looking at courses advertised as B1.

You may find that your level varies when applying different skills. It is not unheard of to be able to speak proficiently at something like a B1 level, but for your writing and reading skills to not be as developed, at A2 or even below. It would then be a good idea to try to bring these skills up to where they should be and invest in a course that is pitched at that level.

When starting out working with a new teacher, it is an enormous help for them to be able to know your existing level. All teachers' courses will to some extent be based on the CEFR scale, and so they will be thinking how best each programme they have prepared can help you. Quoting a CEFR level will tell them far more than anything else about how you feel you fare in the language.

Finally, it's important to know which level you are at in order to avoid gaps opening up. If there are topic areas that you are less confident talking about, but others that you can express yourself fluently on, try working with a course that feels a bit more basic than where you feel you ought to be, in order to make sure that you really have covered all the bases for that level.

How Far Is Far Enough?

C2 is the highest level on the CEFR, and so presents a logical 'end-point' to aim for. However, the truth is that most language learners will never need anything like a C2 level in their chosen language. The degree and depth of knowledge that it requires is simply far beyond what they would ever use the language for.

If you are learning a language to go somewhere on holiday, a B1 level is probably as far as you will ever need to get. The only time when you would want to go further is if perhaps you made friends with local people and wanted to develop your friendship, or were interested in reading newspapers or watching the TV.

To some extent, the level that you will reach in the language is pre-determined by your individual circumstances and personal needs. As these develop and adapt, so too will your need to speak the language better and in a more sophisticated way. But if you find yourself embarking on a course that feels too difficult or that you are lacking the motivation you need to go the extra distance, you have two options: either try to change your circumstances and create a need that will carry you through, or accept that for the time being it simply isn't meant to be.

Improve Your Exam Technique

Tests are a good way to get an objective analysis of your level. However, as is often the case, results tend to depend not just on your knowledge, but also how good you are at demonstrating that knowledge within the confines of an exam.

Language level tests are often set by official boards, which are managed by organisations in the country where the language is spoken. These boards also produce many materials to aid both teachers and students who are to sit the exams. If you are planning to work towards a test, it makes sense to work with the official textbooks that those exam boards produce. All of the material that you find in them will form the basis of the test that you will take. If you learn it all thoroughly, you stand a far better chance of getting a high mark in the exam.

Make sure that you have also read through the mark scheme and are familiar with exactly what the examiners are looking for you to demonstrate at each stage. There will be clear criteria published in order to tell you what you should be working towards. Make sure that you do regular writing practices and record yourself speaking, then use the mark scheme to give yourself a fair self-assessment and see how well you're doing. Your teacher should also be able to help with this.

Ultimately, exams are a chance to show off everything you know in a very short and unnaturally controlled period of time. Whenever you speak or write, you should practise deploying a wide range of different tenses, idioms and expressions, as well as some of the more impressive items of vocabulary that you have learned. All of this helps to create a better impression of you to the examiner, and will show up more favourably in your marks.

TOP TIP: KEEP CALM IN ORAL EXAMS

Oral exams can be a source of much anxiety for language learners. Even if you love speaking the languages you're learning, something about being faced with the examiner can make your heart race, cause you to make mistakes, and end up leaving the wrong impression of your abilities. When entering an exam, remember to keep breathing slowly, smile and relax. If at any point you find yourself getting flustered, take a few seconds to concentrate on your breathing and re-focus yourself on what you're saying. Speak more slowly than you would normally, and everything will run more smoothly. Don't be afraid to pause and think about the words you want to use. Nobody is expecting you to sound like a native speaker, so don't worry about 'dropping the mask' occasionally.

Exercises

....

1. Go to a language school, or find a test online and get an independent assessment of your level in the language you are learning.

2. Find a practice specimen and the mark scheme of the exam you're planning to take. Do the practice exam, and then using the mark scheme assess your score. This will alert you to the kinds of things examiners are looking for when grading papers.

3. Using the mark scheme, record yourself practising the presentation you plan to give in your oral exam and give yourself a mark. Also listen out for any mistakes, any moments of hesitations, or other instances where you sounded unsure. Try to find ways to overcome these when you repeat this exercise.

HOW TO SPEAK ANY LANGUAGE FLUENTLY

Model Answers: Person K

1. After four months of studying Hebrew, Person K's results are at an A1 level. He can have basic conversations and express himself fairly well, but will benefit from a course that will take him to the next level (A2), where he can start talking about more complex issues.

2. Person K realises that he must use more tenses in his writing. The examiners are looking to see that the candidate can write in the past, present and future, even if it feels more 'natural' to just answer a question in the present. He must also try to use more adjectives and find other ways to show off the amount of vocabulary he knows.

3. When listening to his recording, Person K realises that his language sounds quite stilted. He needs to learn more 'connecting' phrases and fillers for when he's pausing, like 'on the other hand', 'but the fact is', 'in my experience', 'according to the experts' etc. Using these makes his speech flow much more naturally and sound more convincing.

CHAPTER 12

Keeping It Going

Learning a new language is like rowing against the current. As soon as you rest your oars, you start floating backwards.

As you reach the goals you set yourself at the start of this book, you may feel that you have done what you set out to achieve and no longer feel as enthusiastic about dedicating yourself to language learning as you once did. The more time that passes, the more words that were once so fresh in your mind will start to fade, and the less comfortable you will feel telling people that you 'speak' the language you've been learning.

Languages get rusty if you don't use them. But if you take the right measures, you can prevent the rust. And that is not as hard as you might think.

Top-Up Days

Schedule these into your calendar every couple of weeks when you're no longer studying regularly. These are your opportunity to reverse the effects of your languages getting rusty.

Use them to:

★ REVIEW

Go back through your materials, re-read passages and remind yourself of vocabulary. If you are using an app like Memrise or Anki, go back through the lists of words you've already learned and make sure they're all fresh in your mind.

★ EXERCISE

Redo some exercises, or find a new grammar workbook that you can dip in and out of on your review days to make sure your memory is still up to date. 'Exercise' can also mean writing and speaking activities, and one-off lessons with a teacher too.

★ LEARN SOMETHING NEW

Pick an article to read about an entirely new topic and make notes on vocabulary as you would normally. Top-up days aren't just about recycling what you already know – use them to make small steps forward as well.

Can You Ever Forget a Language?

It's certainly possible for your level to dip and your progress to start going backwards, but that is not the same as completely forgetting a language, never to recover it again. The new language that you're learning can certainly start to go rusty, but you will never completely undo the hard work that you've put in.

When you feel that your language proficiency is going down, one of the hardest things to do is actually recognising this and doing something about it. This may be because you don't want to fully acknowledge just how bad things have got, or because you remember how much effort it took to get there in the first place, and can't face the idea of going through it all again.

There is good news, though. Learning something for the second time is never as hard as it was the first time. In fact, you're not really learning it again at all. Instead, you're just remembering things that you've already learned, and deep down you've retained them somewhere.

It can take a while to get back into the swing of things, and there will be moments of frustration as you find yourself unable to say the things that once came to you so naturally. However, you will find that you actually remember more than you think. Each memory will link like a chain to another, and slowly you can get it all back. Note, however, that if it has really been a long time since you last looked at the language, then you might need more of a concerted effort than just some top-up days alone.

How to Know Your Language is Getting Rusty

If you fear your language may be in danger of going rusty, here are some clear signs to help you spot it early and act:

★ You can't remember the last time you spoke it.
★ You can remember the last time you spoke it, and it was a disaster.
★ It's been months since you last looked at a language book.
★ Recently when you heard/read your language, you thought, oh, I remember that word!
★ You find yourself exaggerating how well you speak the language to other people.

These are all classic signs that rust is settling. You should be speaking your language regularly, as part of your routine, so it shouldn't be a challenge to think back to when you last used it. And if you can remember when that last time was, you shouldn't feel that you were having more problems using it than normal.

Equally, language books should still be a part of your life. You should still be consulting them, and at least remember the last time you looked at them. If you can't, you probably have been neglecting your skills and they will have started to recede as a result.

When you hear a word and have that minor 'Eureka!' moment of realising you know what it means, unfortunately that is a clear sign that a word you once knew well has started retreating into your passive vocabulary. Although you remember what it means when you heard it, there's no way you would have spontaneously come up with that word by yourself.

Finally, the absolute proof that you're losing grip of your language is if you start talking up your level to other people. When you are regularly studying and learning, you are constantly overwhelmed by the sheer thought of how much you don't know, compared to the tiny amount that you do know. That thought prevents you from ever making bold or brash statements about how good you are, as learning a new language is a process of constantly and repeatedly being humbled. If it looks like you are no longer being humbled, then the likelihood is you're no longer learning.

Review and Revision

Being able to speak a foreign language is really about being in different comfort zones. When you feel that you can speak it well, you have many comfort zones around lots of different topics that you can drift into and out of with ease. As the rust builds up on your language knowledge, these comfort zones start to shrink, which means that you feel less and less comfortable doing the things you always felt able to do.

The first step on the road to recovery is to reclaim those comfort zones. Revise the vocabulary that you need for each topic, and regularly put yourself in a position where you need to use them. That could mean going back to having frequent contact time with a teacher, or reinstating a learning routine.

Beyond that, to prove to yourself that you really are making fresh progress, create new comfort zones too. Start to learn vocabulary for new topics, find articles about things that you haven't studied before, and really focus on the 'learn something new' point from the top-up days mentioned previously.

Don't be ashamed to go back and re-read chapters that you've already completed. There's no such thing as cheating in language learning, as the only way to really make sure you've learned something is to keep revising it. As the saying goes in German: *einmal ist keinmal* (once is never).

Go back and revisit your notes, and don't shy away from making new ones too. You may be able to gain fresh perspectives on topics that you found tricky in the past. That in itself may make it easier for you to relearn some grammar or vocabulary that wouldn't quite stick before.

The Long Game

In today's market for language-learning products, companies place a lot of emphasis on learning fast and with as minimal effort as possible. Many books, courses and products that are available for you to buy will offer to take you through the learning process at breakneck speed, and claim that they are far faster than the so-called 'traditional' approaches. It is true that some of these can achieve this with great success.

However, the faster something is learned, the faster it can be forgotten. It is possible to 'cram' a language, just as you might have crammed for a test or exam while you were at school. The knowledge will stay with you for as long as you need it to, but the moment your need subsides, everything will promptly be lost again.

If your long-term objective is to speak this language not just in the short term, but to continue speaking it well into the future and for many years to come, you should view these miracle products with a healthy dose of scepticism. Ask yourself if there really is a rush to cram the language you are learning, and if not, you should feel free to take more time over it. Like that, you can be sure that what you are learning will stay with you for far longer than if you were to whizz through it without stopping.

This approach supports the view given in Chapter 2 on time management. You should view your language learning holistically, as something that you achieve over the course of many months, years and even a lifetime. Whether or not you reach a certain degree of fluency in just a couple of months really is beside the point. What actually matters is whether or not the time that you invest into your language study pays off in the longer term. You should be making sure that the skills and experiences that you gain over the course of the learning process stay with you well into the future.

Languages and Socialising

One of the best ways to ensure that you're able to keep up your language learning in the long term is to design a lifestyle and routine that is centred around it. You can do this by finding new friends and socialising with people who also share your passion for languages.

Unfortunately, learning languages is likely to always remain a relatively niche hobby, but that does not mean that it has to be an isolating one. Whether you know it or not, many people of all different backgrounds share your enjoyment and love of learning languages, and would be delighted to meet others who feel the same way. Knowing other people who are learning languages is extremely motivating, and can lead to you setting up new language exchanges with people, and make sure that you all keep working towards your language-learning objectives.

There are many different events organised in cities around the world, designed to connect people who like learning languages. There are many language-specific meetup events available through social media and Meetup.com, but also ones that are more generally there for people who love languages.

The largest of these is the Polyglot Conference, which since 2013 has attracted language enthusiasts from all over the world, and each year continues to grow and be held in different locations around the world. It also offers talks by world-leading experts on topics to do with multilingualism and others that will be of innate interest to everybody who loves language.

For those who are unable to travel, social media now offers a plethora of groups and places to meet virtually with other enthusiasts online, as mentioned in Chapter 9.

Learning More Languages

If you really loved the experience of learning your first foreign language, there is no reason why you should stop there.

It may well be time for you to start thinking about learning your second one! There are literally thousands of languages out there in the world, which means over the course of a lifetime you will never run out of new ones to learn, and new worlds to explore.

Many people like to learn about languages as a way of fuelling a deeper interest in linguistics. Indeed, many linguists can tell you an awful lot of facts about the grammar and structure of languages, even though they might not necessarily be able to speak them.

However, if your goal is to develop a level of proficiency in speaking multiple languages, then all of the processes described in this book will easily apply once more. You should pick a language that you have a clear and unequivocal motivation to learn, and plan strategically how you approach it.

The most important question to ask, though, is when the right moment is to start looking towards your next language. This is critical, as if you move too quickly, you run the risk of losing the language you have previously been studying. Your knowledge of it may not yet be in-depth enough to withstand learning another one, as you open your mind to an onslaught of new information.

You should certainly not start learning a new language until you have reached the objective you set out to achieve with your first one. This way, you will be ensuring that you are not simply 'replacing' one language with another, but really are adding to it.

Juggling Multiple Different Languages

One of the most common concerns about learning more than one language is how to avoid getting them mixed up. It can be extremely humiliating to try to speak one language, but ending up saying words in a totally different one.

You will always run the risk of having the occasional crossed wire between the different languages that you know. However, with practice, patience, and a degree of technique, avoiding mixing up different languages is a skill that you can definitely develop.

Here are some things to think about:

★ DON'T LEARN SIMILAR LANGUAGES STRAIGHT AWAY

If, for example, you've just been learning Spanish, the worst thing you can do is immediately start learning Portuguese. These languages are far too similar in terms of their grammar, their vocabulary and their pronunciation for you to guarantee that you won't mix them up, or just learn one as a feigned accent in the other. Instead, you might want to think about French, which is still very similar to Spanish, but different enough for you to feel like you are learning a different language.

★ ALWAYS FOCUS ON MAKING ONE LANGUAGE YOUR BEST

The better you know a language, the less likely you are to make blunders. If you do want to learn a very similar language to the one you've already learned, it's worth holding off until you feel confident enough to really feel fluent in the first one. That means something like a C1 or C2 level. Hyperpolyglot Richard Simcott, one of the UK's most multilingual people who has studied over thirty different languages, likes to think of these as 'anchor languages', and advises that it's best to have one in each language family (e.g. Romance, Germanic, Slavic, Semitic, etc.) before trying to learn others.

★ CONFRONT ANY SIMILARITIES HEAD ON

In the event that you have just been learning Spanish and now absolutely have to learn Italian, the best strategy is to look at the two languages side by side and force yourself to take their many similarities and differences head-on. You may want to try taking an Italian class full of Spanish speakers, as this will help you to really hear the differences and ensure you don't waste time trying to learn common grammar points that you already know from Spanish. Alternatively, you could find textbooks and courses that are designed for native Spanish speakers, as these will very clearly explain the similarities and also focus on highlighting the differences, while showing you how you can deal with them.

★ TRAIN YOURSELF TO SWITCH

It's always extremely impressive to see someone seamlessly switching in and out of multiple different languages in conversations. However, it is never as easy as it looks. Switching languages is a skill that you have to develop. Start training yourself to be more flexible by scheduling lessons or planning study periods for different languages, one straight after the other, to get used to switching. Also, try keeping multilingual vocabulary lists, in which you write a new word out in all of the different languages that you are learning. That way, you can maintain your different languages and help prevent one of your languages from becoming significantly better than the others. Ultimately, though, remember that while switching in and out of languages is a good trick and will impress people at parties, in actual fact you will rarely need to be able to move in and out of different languages so quickly in one go. You will have phases in which you find yourself needing one language more than any other, which gives you time and plenty of warning to warm it up first.

TOP TIP: LADDERING

One technique favoured by polyglots who speak many different languages is 'laddering', or learning one language through another. This 'kill two birds with one stone' approach allows you to have contact with the language of instruction, in which all grammar explanations and instructions is given, while also learning the language that is being taught. Apart from anything, this technique will really broaden your horizons in terms of materials that you can use. Many of the world's best language-learning resources are written in languages other than English. If you are able to read languages like French, German or even Russian, that will be a huge help in accessing some of the world's lesser documented languages.

Final Thoughts

Language learning really does never stop. There are enough languages in the world to last you several different lifetimes, and within those languages you will never be short of new challenges, fresh perspectives, and the chance to come across new things at all stages of life. Learning languages is an extremely satisfying, endlessly useful and very applicable hobby. Whatever else you wish to do in life, the ability to speak another language can only be an asset to you. As you gain more experience with languages, you will get to better understand your individual learning style, and work out which techniques work best for you, and even adapt them to develop your own.

A word of warning though: learning languages, discovering new cultures and meeting new people is a highly addictive and immensely exciting way to live your life. Once you have a taste for languages, it's hard to imagine life without them.

I wish you the best of luck!

Index

HOW TO SPEAK ANY LANGUAGE FLUENTLY

HOW TO SPEAK ANY LANGUAGE FLUENTLY